The
Power
of Your Life
Message

Decisions That Define Us

By David Crone

DESTINY IMAGE₀ PUBLISHERS, INC.
P.O. Box 310, Shippensburg, PA 17257-0310

"Speaking to the Purposes of God for This Generation and for the Generations to Come."

This book and all other Destiny Image, Revival Press, MercyPlace, Fresh Bread, Destiny Image Fiction, and Treasure House books are available at Christian bookstores and distributors worldwide.

For a U.S. bookstore nearest you, call 1-800-722-6774.
For more information on foreign distributors, call 717-532-3040.
Reach us on the Internet: www.destinyimage.com.

Trade Paper ISBN 13: 978-0-7684-3274-9
Hardcover ISBN 13: 978-0-7684-3503-0
Large Print ISBN 13: 978-0-7684-3504-7
Ebook ISBN 13: 978-0-7684-9091-6

For Worldwide Distribution, Printed in the U.S.A.

1 2 3 4 5 6 7 8 9 10 11 / 13 12 11 10

Dedication

To Deborah, my childhood sweetheart and lifelong companion. To my children: Jeremy, my firstborn, a man with the courage to fight for the greater good; Ryan, my armor bearer, a man with a heart like God's; Amy, my greatest fan, who now cheers me on from the grandstand of the great cloud of witnesses. To my parents, who not only gave me life but handed me a legacy worth living up to.

Acknowledgment

I want to thank the company of believers, dreamers, and friends who call The Mission home. Their adventurous spirit continues to amaze me. I also wish to say thank you to the leadership team Deborah and I are privileged to walk with. Their friendship, encouragement, and love have been life giving on this journey of discovery.

Endorsements

Last year at our Leaders Advance, David and Deborah Crone shared with 800 of our leaders how God had given them a family creed that would be passed through their generational linage, laying a foundation for their legacy. We were all stunned; some were weeping quietly while others were motionless on the floor, desperately trying to capture the depth of this revelation. All of us could sense this defining moment in our personal history...a porthole into timeless thinking.

Months later David sent me this manuscript and asked me to endorse it. As I read through the pages of the book, I couldn't believe what my eyes were seeing and my heart was feeling...he had somehow managed to capture this same revelational experience on paper!

In this amazing book, *The Power Of Your Life Message,* David Crone takes us from the mind-sets of mere commoners to the ways of nobleman. This book WILL change your life. It is a "must read" for every believer.

Kris Vallotton, Senior Associate Leader
Bethel Church, Redding, California
Author of several books including,
The Supernatural Ways Of Royalty

The fourth wall is the imaginary "wall" that exists between the audience and the actors on the stage, through which the audience sees the action in the world of the play. When this boundary is "broken" by an actor on the stage speaking directly to the audience, it is called "breaking the fourth wall."

In his book, *The Power of Your Life Message*, David Crone has broken the fourth wall. While enveloped in the pain and grief of having lost his daughter, David has chosen to embrace God's grace and speak directly to us. His words are not the prepared and practiced speech of the actor, the politician, or the theologian. They are not words learned in a classroom. They are words laced with the lessons learned as he and Deborah have walked through tragedy and disappointment. They did not hang their harps on the willow tree. They made a choice, a decision to continue to sing the Lord's song. As David has poignantly spoken, our decisions define us and determine what our life message will be.

Barry McGuire wrote the words to this song a long time ago.

> I walked a mile with sorrow.
> Never a word said she.
> But oh the things I learned
> When sorrow walked with me.

In reading David's book I have found courage and hope to live my own life as a sign of God's glory and grace. It is a great honor to recommend this book to you. Read it with an open heart. There is much you will learn from his life message. His words will help you to write your own story.

Don Milam
VP, Destiny Image Publishers
Author, *The Ancient Language of Eden*

Table of Contents

Foreword
by Bill Johnson

A number of years ago, I heard a story about the trouble logging companies were having keeping their logs from being stolen. After the trees were freshly cut, the logs would be stacked and marked at both ends with paint or a steel punch to show the company's brand. The problem came about when there was a competing company nearby that was dishonest. All they had to do was cut off each end of the log and re-mark it as one of their own. That all ended when someone invented a device that would brand the log with a laser beam. After the log was in place, one of the workers would attach this device to the end of a log, and it would mark the center of the log throughout its entire length. That meant it didn't matter where you cut the log, the brand of that particular company would be seen.

I've known David Crone for many years, and he is much like that branded log. No matter where you look into his life, the brand of God's purpose is there. He is a man of uncompromising devotion to the heart of God. It is his life's message. His continual preference for others reveals that this contagious passion burns not only for himself, but also for everyone around him.

It is hard to be with David for long before one wonders how he can improve awareness of God's purpose for his life. David has that effect. *The Power of Your Life Message* is a profound book that will thrill the reader with insight and motivation. I found myself laughing out loud on one page, and my eyes filled with tears on another. It is rich with truth, overflowing with wisdom, and profound in its attention to what matters most to God. Please read this book *without* caution, and be ready to burn with divine passion and ready to receive the intimate touch of a loving Father. Read it for the adventure…and let's together fulfill the plan of God for this generation.

Bill Johnson
Senior Pastor Bethel Church, Redding, CA
Author of *When Heaven Invades Earth* and *Face to Face with God*

Foreword
by Graham Cooke

*W*e are all living with the sense that the place where we are living spiritually is too small to accommodate the majesty of God's Presence. This is true of us on a personal as well as corporate level.

Increase is important to God. He can only really be glorified in fullness. We have no choice regarding an abundant lifestyle. We live with a Father who fills all things with Himself.

If it were simply a matter of filling up the internal space that we currently have available, then, no problem, let's go for it. That however, is not enough to satisfy God's innate generosity. As well as filling us, He must of necessity expand our hearts, minds, and spirit so that we are becoming large enough in grace to live a multiplied lifestyle of favor.

Enlargement is the order of the day and the lifeblood of the Kingdom. We are doing life business with magnificence. We must be made in His image and He is not small!

The Father commits us to an ever-increasing lifestyle of growth through the events and circumstances that He allows and often engineers around us. In those joyful, painful, wonderful, and difficult situations He teaches us a way of being with Him that is constant and consistent. He imparts

His own unchanging nature to us and, by grace, empowers us to be as He is in this world.

He teaches us the values of Heaven and their importance on Earth as a carrier of His presence. He brings the influence of His own internal community to bear upon our life and relationships. God offered the gift of oneness to people when He created them.

He lives in a community of Father, Son, and Holy Spirit. Oneness is intrinsic to His very Being. We are designed to reflect the image of Oneness and shared community. Community therefore is God's highest aim. *"That they might be one, as we are one"* (John 17: 21-23). Community is deeply grounded in the nature of God. It is the place where He influences who we are and how we live. We make decisions, life choices in the light of the people He puts around us. No man is an island. Our destiny is shared through oneness and togetherness. Our legacy flows out of community.

Community is family, friendships, business, church... indeed, any group dynamic can share in the oneness created by involvement with the Kingdom of Heaven. Jesus and the disciples were a mobile community creating an environment of oneness wherever they went.

Relationships are about the impact we have on one another for good. The currency of community is goodness: *"So then, while we have opportunity, let us do good to all people and especially to those who are of the household of faith"* (Gal. 6:10). Goodness provides a focus that governs life.

All these things are at the heart of how David and Deborah live. They are the passions that they thrive on. David's life message flows out of community. In life we are presented with options and priorities and we must learn the difference. Priorities are nonnegotiable. We live our life in a given way. Our heart is fixed.

The values of Heaven form the priorities of life. God is intentional toward us. He is consistent. His faithfulness is everlasting.

David's commitment to "Non Inferiora Secutus" is inspirational to those of us privileged to be in community with him. His passion to allow others to grow and succeed at their own life messages has allowed our community to develop an atmosphere of goodness and love that is impactful for all of us. God loves to change us from glory to glory. Life in the Spirit is always better than at our beginnings. Our identity is held firmly in the heart of God. Our life message is upgraded continually as we journey into a deeper relationship with the God of community.

David's book is the story of how to journey with God in the development of a life message big enough to accommodate majesty. We are surrounded by the community of Heaven, impacted by the oneness of God.

The excellence of Jesus will not allow us to live below the line of destiny spoken. Our personal negativity about ourselves cannot prevent the Lord from overwhelming us with His goodness. When God says "Nevertheless," He is not willing for us to settle for less. Fullness is our way of life, not measure.

We must put ourselves in the way of God and His resourcing. It is time for an upgrade in our life message. As you read the story of David and Deborah's journey, take time to get your own story straight and your own journey back on track.

You are much too important to be inferior and you are more beloved than you know. Destiny is waiting for you to upgrade your identity. Your life message is vital to your life and the lives of all those you are meant to influence.

Graham Cooke
Friend of David Crone

Introduction

A man's journey is both personal and communal. No one can live it for him, yet he cannot live it alone. The road he chooses to travel does much to shape his character, personality, and passion, while at the same time it influences the community around him. This was certainly true of my spiritual journey—especially in the last ten years. I'm sure it was true before then, but I was not as acutely aware of it as I am now.

My wife, Deborah, and I have often tried to put into words just what happened to us that so radically changed our approach to life and faith. One thing we are sure of is that it started where all things good and wonderful are initiated— with God. Our dissatisfaction with church life after 25 years of vocational ministry, our cry for authentic Christianity, even our increased hunger for His manifest presence all began in the heart of the Father.

In a more pictorial way, I would describe our transformation as a "coming out." We had lived in a safe and practical room filled with family and friends, enjoying the belief that God was predictable and the Holy Spirit was always a gentleman. Our doctrine was sure, our values were in place, and our interpretation of Scripture was unquestionable. We had all the right passages in Scripture underlined—you know, the ones that supported what we believed. We were sure that the room we were in was all there was to the Kingdom of God, and yet our hearts began to question the truth of it.

Then God chose to answer the cry He had put in our hearts and opened a door, inviting us to explore the rest of the house. We didn't hesitate—we were ready for a coming-out party.

What a party it has been. As we followed the leading of the Holy Spirit, we discovered that the room we had been in most of our lives was just a small part of God's Kingdom. There were rooms filled with signs that made us wonder and revelations of the goodness of God that overwhelmed us. Each day we made new discoveries about the God we had loved and served since we were children. Worship took its proper place and became a lifestyle. We began to see the power of God manifested in and through our lives, and in the lives of those around us. Old values that had no connection to true principles began to fall away. God became more real than ever, and the Scriptures took on new life. We have experienced the love of the Father, the brotherhood of the Son, and the friendship of the Holy Spirit in ever-increasing dimensions, and we are still finding new rooms filled with more of the things that God has prepared for those who love Him.

This adventure of discovering the King and His Kingdom has had both personal and community impact. The stories and thoughts found in the chapters of this book are just some of the things we have discovered in this journey over the last ten or so years. They have changed the way we think and branded us in very personal ways, becoming a part of our life message. They have also molded the way the community called "The Mission" goes about church life. As you read through this book, you will see our personal journey inter-woven with the journey of our family and the community of believers we have been privileged to live with.

My hope is that as you read this book, you will have your own "coming out" party and discover the many rooms God has ready and waiting for you. It is also my prayer that this book will help you find, if you have not yet discovered them, the words that will give transforming power to the message of your life.

SECTION ONE

The Value

The first section of this book looks at the importance of one's life message. Each chapter speaks to the value of discovering, developing, and pursuing the true message of your life and gives helpful insights into the process.

CHAPTER ONE

Non Inferiora Secutus

"To escape criticism—do nothing, say nothing, be nothing."
—Elbert Hubbard

A life message is more than a passion, and different from a dream or vision. A life message can be heard in what we say, seen in how we live, and is reflected in the decisions we make. It resonates in the core of our being, yet it is often easier for others to identify and articulate for us. Some people recognize their life message, verbalize it well, nurture it and use it as a compass for their destiny. Others fail to see it and don't capitalize on its value.

Joshua declared his life message when he stated, *"but as for me and my house, we will serve the Lord"* (Josh. 24:15 NASB). This was more than just a slogan that he developed for a motivational pep talk. Its message is foundational in every recorded experience of his life. Joshua demonstrated this core decision the day he stood with Caleb and contradicted the faithless testimony of the eight other spies. It is further evident in his faithful vigilance outside the tent of the presence of God. By the time he stood before the children of Israel near the end of his life, *"as for me and my house…"* erupted out of who he had always been.

In over 30 years of pastoral ministry, I have stood over the graveside of many people and listened as family members and friends spoke of the life message of their loved one. Each time I have privately asked, "What will people say about me when I'm the one in the grave? What will be the message of my life that my children, grandchildren, and life-long friends will speak of?" I have also wondered if I will know the message of my life well enough while alive to nurture its development and reap its benefits.

Taken by Surprise

I was a prenatal church attendee. My mom and dad rarely missed a service and seldom failed to take my sister and me along. I slept under more chairs and church pews than I can remember. Thankfully, my parents lived what they believed. We were part of quality churches led by wonderful men whose lives matched their ministries. It was an easy, but genuine, decision for me to give my life to Christ and follow after Him. At the age of seven, I made a public confession of my faith, though Christ had been a reality in my heart for a long time. My journey with God has been a life-long pursuit.

This adventure with God has shaped what I have become and continues to form what I am becoming. Along the way, there have been many significant road markers in the process of developing my life message, but none more important than the day I discovered a statement which put that message into words.

Deborah and I were spending a few days of rest in a quaint community in northern California. While there, we came across a shop that was selling clothing and decorative items from Scotland and Ireland. Having an interest in Celtic history and culture, we wandered in and looked around.

A book of family crests and mottos lay on one of the counters. I began to leaf through it with moderate interest, until my gaze rested on the motto of the Buchan family from Scotland, and I was suddenly captivated and overwhelmed by what I read: "Non Inferiora Secutus—not having followed inferior things."

I was "gob-smacked," as one of my English friends puts it, speechless and astounded by the radical resolve of this Scottish clan, and by how it resonated in the deep places of my heart. Every part of my being was shaken by the impact of these words. My knees buckled and I was shaking so much, I had to lean against the counter to remain upright. I motioned for Deborah to come over to the counter, and after pointing out the book, I excused myself and went outside, hoping that some fresh air would help me get a grip on my emotions and control the physical manifestations. It didn't help; I was in the grip of a God encounter and my being could not contain it.

I ended up out on the sidewalk leaning against a lamp post like a drunken man. It took all of that day before I could reflect on those words without becoming emotionally and physically undone. Their impact resonates in me even now as I recall the story.

SCRIPTURAL CONTEXT

Shortly after this experience, I was reading the Book of Philippians in *The Message Bible* when I came across these words:

> *I gave up all that inferior stuff so I could know Christ personally, experience his resurrection power, be a partner in his suffering, and go all the way with him to death itself....I've got my eye on the goal, where God is beckoning us onward—to Jesus. I'm off and running and I'm not turning back* (Philippians 3:10-13 TM).

I was convinced that "Non Inferiora Secutus" was God's idea and a description of my life journey.

NIS, initials for the Latin phrase "Non Inferiora Secutus," has become our family motto and our individual life quest. When I shared NIS with my family, we all agreed that this motto puts into words the way we desire to live our lives and what we want to leave as a legacy. NIS is not to us a casual slogan or cute expression. It is a commitment to a journey into all that is superior, that which exceeds the norm and requires exceptional faith and character. It is our way of saying we are seeking first the Kingdom of God, we are reaching for the goal of fulfilling the call of God on our lives, and we are not turning back.

Over the past several years, we have kept this message in front of our eyes to constantly remind us of the call and the commitment to hold ourselves and each other accountable to the truth expressed on this insignia. We do this in a number of creative ways. My sons and I wear a ring bearing the NIS crest, and my daughters and Deborah have bracelets and necklaces that also carry the NIS insignia. Family businesses have it in their business name; we put it on our car license plates; we use it in our email addresses. A plaque hangs in each of our homes that includes the verse from Philippians 3 and reads:

> The wearers of these rings covenant together to never walk in inferior paths, choose inferior goals, or settle for inferior character. Each will aspire, with the help of God and each other, to reach for the greatest good in all things pertaining to faith and life.

AN NIS SEA CAPTAIN

People are constantly asking me what NIS means when they see it on my car or ring. It is a great way to share my faith and to encourage others in their life pursuits.

I was talking with a friend from Australia, Colon Brown, a few months ago when he asked the inevitable question: "What does NIS stand for?" As I explained that it was a family crest that we adopted from the Buchan family, he excitedly stated, "I'm from the Buchan family. My great, great grandfather, John Buchan, came to Australia as a sea captain in the late 1800s." I became very interested to hear more, especially to hear if the family—or at least this one member of the family, John—actually lived what their motto declared. I was encouraged to discover that John Buchan was authentic to his family's life message. The following is a summary of John Buchan's story taken from the family records that Colon emailed to me, one man's expression of NIS:

John Buchan was born 1834 in the village of Inveral-lochy on the Northeast coast of Scotland. He describes his home this way:

> My home was humble, but ennobled by Christ's presence. And as His love was the ruling Spirit in it, there was more true happiness, than there is in the mansions of the world's favorite worldlings.

John's childhood became difficult when his father died of cholera and 12 months later his mother simply stopped breathing, leaving the children parentless. The children were passed among family relatives; at the age of 16 John took to the sea as a cabin boy.

Life on a sailing vessel was hard and offered an inferior way of living. Many times John had to make the choice between the immoral lifestyles of his fellow seaman or the way of Christ. Sometimes he faced the choice between loyalty and personal advancement. As difficult as these choices were, John wavered little in his commitment to NIS. His choice to not follow inferior ways was often met with ridicule and poor treatment from his colleagues. However, it was not unusual for one of them to come to him in private and express their repentance and inquire regarding John's way of living. John's authentic lifestyle was many times rewarded with promotion and favor from those in authority.

Near the end of John's life he wrote the following:

> Believing that my life is precarious and may end suddenly, I wish to place on record the following confession:

> That death has no terror for me. The religion which I have professed since I was 20 or 21 years of age,

is no mere theory, based on external evidences, and such that could be overthrown by counter-evidences; it is a matter of the heart, and is beyond the reach of all the attacks of unbelief, scepticism, and infidelity. Ever since I knew the Lord as my Saviour, I could say with Paul, "I **know** whom I have believed." Belief in the love that made the Son of God suffer for me, creates the response which forms our everlasting bond of union; and now I can with confidence say "who (or what) shall separate us?"

His service, though performed in a humble way, has brightened my life, and I am cheered by the hope of having the privilege of serving Him in the world to come.

John Buchan
September 7, 1908

CHAPTER TWO

A Life of Discovery

"The music is all around us. All you have to do is listen."
—August Rush

*D*iscovery plays a big part in developing and identifying one's life message. In my journey, the discovery of NIS was one of hundreds, if not thousands, of personal discoveries that have helped me unwrap the things God declares I am. It should be no surprise to any of us that God hides things so we can find them. He creates the ultimate Easter egg hunt. He wants us to uncover things about ourselves, our world, His Kingdom, and—most importantly— things about Him. Discovering God and His Kingdom is truly the great, never-ending, divine journey. Each aspect of God's character and nature is an eternal adventure of its own. It's a good thing eternity has no time constraints.

Revelation is the revealing of something that is already there—but not known until the moment of discovery. Revealed truth is not a truth that never before existed, but a truth that has been hidden from us until uncovered.

Hidden Treasure

A couple of months ago, I was reading a news article about the discovery of the wreckage of the 400-ton *Quedagh Merchant* off the coast of Catalina Island in the Dominican Republic. The Armenian vessel was captured by the infamous Captain Kidd on January 30, 1698, in the Indian Ocean, and was considered to be his greatest prize. He renamed the ship the *Adventure Prize*.

In 1699, Captain Kidd was forced to leave the *Adventure Prize* in the Caribbean, while he made his way to New York in a futile attempt to clear his name of piracy. The vessel was looted and then scuttled by the crew he left behind.

Treasure hunters have searched for this famous ship for centuries without success, until a local diver stumbled across it just a few months ago. Archaeologists from the University of Indiana were amazed to find that the wreck had remained undisturbed by looters for over 300 years.

The thing that fascinated me was that the ship was discovered in this unmolested state just 70 feet from shore, in ten feet of crystal-clear water. It was there all the time waiting for someone to find it, someone whose heart was set on discovery.

I have often wondered if I discovered NIS or it discovered me. Or was it both? Could it be that this life-transforming thought was an expression looking for a heart and I was a heart looking for an expression? I don't know the answer to that question, but I do know that on the day I read those words, they so resonated in my being that it felt as if an entire orchestra had struck the downbeat of Beethoven's Fifth. I had found an expression for the beat of my heart, and it continues to influence my every decision and action.

SURPRISE REVELATIONS

A revelation that expresses the message of one's life can be discovered in unexpected places and at unexpected times. For me, it was in a Celtic shop on a side street in the foothills of California, waiting for my wife to finish shopping. For Jacob, it was in a wide spot in the road called Luz at a time when gaining revelation was the last thing on his mind.

Jacob was on his way to his uncle's family, having been sent there by his mother to find a wife. On top of wondering what this woman was going to look like or what kind of personality she would have, he had other things pressing for his attention. He had left his hometown under a cloud and finding a wife wasn't the only reason for the trip. Jacob's mother, Rebekah, thought it was a good time for Jacob to skip town and get away from his brother Esau, who was having thoughts of killing Jacob for stealing his birthright.

As you can see, Jacob had plenty to occupy his mind when he chose to make camp at Luz. Yet it was at Luz that Jacob would have an experience that would set him on a path of discovering his true identity.

It was at Luz, on his way to find a wife and get away from his brother, that God confirmed to Jacob the promises He had made to Jacob's grandfather and father, Abraham and Isaac, and spoke the words that would be his prophetic destiny:

> *I am the LORD God of Abraham your father and the God of Isaac; the land on which you lie I will give to you and your descendants. Also your descendants shall be as the dust of the earth; you shall spread abroad to the west and the east, to the north and the south; and in you and in your seed all the families of the earth shall be blessed. Behold, I am with you and will keep you wherever you go, and will bring you back to this land; for I will not leave you until I have done what I have spoken to you* (Genesis 28:13-15).

Jacob's response seems somewhat humorous to me and reveals the unexpected timing of the revelation:

> *Surely the LORD is in this place, and I did not know it…How awesome is this place! This is none other than the house of God, and this is the gate of heaven!* (Genesis 28:16,17)

Jacob was so impacted by this revelation that he changed the name of the town to Bethel, meaning the house of God, and Bethel would remain an important place for the rest of Jacob's life.

It would not be the last defining moment of Jacob's life in a place and time he didn't expect it. At Peniel on his way to make peace with his brother, he would wrestle with God, his name would be changed to Israel, and he would never walk the same again.

Unexpected places at unexpected times are perfect hiding spaces for life-defining discoveries. They are there to be found by those who recognize them when they seemingly stumble into them.

Hidden in Plain Sight

They can also be found in familiar places, places you can expect revelation but often don't discover it, because they are so familiar. I wonder how many times the fishermen from the Dominican Republic cast their nets over the wreck of Captain Kidd's ship but never saw it? How many snorkelers and boaters looked into the crystal-clear waters of the Caribbean, 70 feet off the shore of Catalina Island, yet failed to recognize the treasure that was just ten feet below them?

When I talk to people about their life message I often get a response that indicates that they don't believe they have one, or have not been able to identify language that defines it. My first question is, "Do you have a favorite Scripture, one that resonates with your spirit more than others?" Invariably the answer is an emphatic "Yes." Often, a familiar verse of Scripture is an important part of the language for your life message and a familiar place to begin your discovery.

When I share this idea with some people, a light of revelation often comes on and they talk about how a particular Scripture has been passed down from generation to generation in their family—a scripture such as, *"As for me and my house, we will serve the Lord"* (Josh. 24:15). They go on to share that they now can see how the message of that Scripture has been reflected in the way the generations have conducted their lives. Their life message was hidden for their discovery in a familiar place all the time. All they had to do was look with new eyes and listen with new ears.

HAVING EARS TO HEAR

Samuel came to this discovery in the familiar place of service. Samuel was dedicated by his mother to serve God in the temple from the time he was a young child. As a part of his service, he ministered to Eli, the priest. Eli was an old man, and I am sure he called upon Samuel at all hours of the day and night to help him in very common things.

In this place of familiar service, one night Samuel heard what he assumed was the voice of Eli calling him once again. He responded as he always had by getting out of bed and going to the priest's side, offering his aid. This time Eli's response must have been curious to Samuel. Eli told him he had not called him. This happened two more times, each time with the same result. Samuel was beginning to think the old man was becoming senile when Eli realized what was happening and instructed him that it was God that was talking to him and to answer Him the next time he heard the voice. Up to this time, Samuel was not familiar with the voice of the Lord, but because he heard it in a familiar setting, he interpreted it in the usual way and missed that it was God.

The next time Samuel heard the voice, he listened with new ears and the words of the Lord set him on his destiny as a prophet of God. How many wonders of the Kingdom, and revelations about ourselves and our God may have remained hidden to us because we saw them in familiar places, masquerading as ordinary?

Treasure in Others' Fields

One of these ordinary places is in another man's field. Jesus gave us a parable describing the Kingdom of God. He tells the story of a man who finds a treasure in another man's field, and he so values it that he sells all he has to purchase the field and acquire the treasure. The man did what was necessary to appropriate it as his own.

I consider myself a very wealthy man because of the people God has allowed me to have as mentors, friends, and colleagues. Much of the treasure I have has been discovered in their fields—shared in phone conversations or chats at Peets Coffee, or casual conversations at meals, ballgames, and staff meetings. All ordinary places with people that could easily be taken for granted because they are everywhere around me.

Deborah, the woman God gave me, is a deep well of wisdom and revelation. If I am not paying attention, she will say something I need to hear and I will miss it—it's in a field that is familiar. Familiarity does not have to breed contempt for us to miss out on some of the great jewels of the Kingdom. All it need do is dull our appreciation for the treasure that is in the fields of the people around us.

Allow me to offer a caution here. Finding treasure in another man's field doesn't mean much until we buy the field and appropriate it for ourselves. In the context of this chapter, let me suggest that to *buy the field* means to do more than hear the revelation and say, "that's a good word." Rather, it is to process the word into our lives in cooperation with the Holy Spirit until it becomes who we are. We will die of hunger if all we do is smell our food, and we will never have the hidden treasure until we buy the field.

Hidden in the Clutter

Another place where we can look for revelatory treasure is in the clutter of our lives. Jesus again gave us a story that illustrates this hiding place. He said there was a woman who lost a valuable coin. This coin was one of a set of ten that would represent today a stone in a wedding band. It had value to this woman beyond the worth of the coin itself. The parable goes on to tell that the woman lit a lamp, swept out the house, and searched until she found the coin. She found her valued treasure among the clutter of her house.

There are lost treasures from our past that have fallen into the clutter of our lives through neglect. Some of these jewels are revelations that we received, but the things of life have overshadowed them and we have allowed clutter to hide them from our present understanding. But there is good news; they are still there ready to be rediscovered by partnering with the Holy Spirit and giving Him permission to shine His light in the rooms of our inner house and sweep out the corners until the treasure is exposed. His focus is the treasure, not the clutter.

Recently the Holy Spirit helped me see this in a fresh way through a physical illustration. My daughter says that I have three places where I pile things—where I've been, where I am, and where I'm going. She is accurate, as I "file by pile." In order to find anything, I have to clean up the piles.

The other day I was on such a search when I went into a drawer in my desk that was full of a variety of things. As I cleared out the clutter, I did not find what I was looking for but I found a treasure that meant even more. Hidden in the back of the drawer was a South African Krugerrand that Curt Klein, a colleague at The Mission, gave me years ago as a means of encouragement during a time when my faith was being tested.

In finding the gold in the clutter of that drawer, I not only recovered the monetary value of the item that had been lost to me, but even better, I once again received the benefit of the original encouragement. Treasures that will help us define our life message are awaiting us in the places of clutter.

RIGHT WHERE YOU EXPECT IT

Before I conclude this chapter, allow me to point out one other place where you can discover life-changing revelation. It is in the expected places.

What I mean by the expected places is this: there are times when we intentionally go after revelation, positioning ourselves to receive that revelation, and in those times we can expect to find it. These are times of prayer and meditating on Scripture, times when we purposefully listen to the Holy Spirit, times when we give ourselves to worship and thanksgiving, and times in community when we set ourselves to hear the word taught.

These times and places are where we can expect to discover truth about God, His Kingdom, and ourselves. We can expect it because God has promised it. He has made it very clear that those who seek Him will find Him, those who knock will get an answer, and those who ask will receive what they ask for.

One of my favorite movies is *August Rush*. It is the story of a young boy named Evan Taylor, searching for the parents he never knew. He is harassed by the boys in his orphanage because he believes he hears a sound that will lead him to his parents.

One day he decides to follow the sound and runs away into the big city of New York. There he is taken under the cruel wing of a musician named Wizard, who has collected a group of orphaned children talented in music and uses them on the streets to perform for money. They all live in a condemned opera house in the inner city.

Wizard discovers that Evan is a musical genius. Wizard, in a veiled attempt to hide Evan's true identity and give him a more marketable image, changes Evan's name to August Rush.

August confides in Wizard that he hears a sound everywhere he goes, and he asks Wizard: "Where do you think it comes from, what I hear?"

Wizard responds: "It comes from all around...It's invisible..."

Evan: "So only some of us can hear it?"

Wizard: "Only some of us are listening."[1]

PAY ATTENTION

Are you looking to discover the authentic message of your life? Are you searching for language that will help communicate the passion of your heart in a way that gives you a compass for your journey? Look first and continually in the expected places. Ask the Holy Spirit to reveal your heart and tune it to His. Then you will have ears that hear and eyes that see in the unexpected places, the familiar and ordinary settings, all the places the Father has 'hidden' His secrets for you to find. You and I were meant to be discoverers and adventurers in the Kingdom of God, to be those who hear what others don't and see what others can't.

August Rush begins with the voice of the 11-year-old Evan speaking over the sound of the opening music: "Can you hear it? The Music? I can hear it everywhere in the wind, in the air, in the light. It's all around us. All you have to do is open yourself up. All you have to do is listen."

The movie ends in a similar fashion. August has freed himself from Wizard and found his parents. He is conducting the New York Philharmonic orchestra in Central Park as they perform his original music. As the music fades and the camera pans away from the park, August's voice is the last thing you hear saying, "The music is all around us. All you have to do is listen."[2]

There is a life message for us to discover. It is a message that will empower us in our prophetic destiny and maximize our life's impact. The music of our life message is all around us. Let's set our heart to discover it, and tune our ears to hear it.

ENDNOTES

1. Excerpts from *August Rush* granted courtesy of Warner Bros. Entertainment Inc.

2. Ibid.

CHAPTER THREE

The Tale of Two Lives

"You make a living by what you earn. You make a life by what you give."—Winston Churchill

A person's life message acts as a compass for three important elements that make up our contribution to the world around us. These elements are influence, destiny, and legacy. One's life message keeps these components pointed true north and enhances their quality.

INFLUENCE

Influence is the power that indirectly or intangibly affects a person or a course of events. It is the effect we have on others and the atmosphere around us. Influence is different from reputation. It is the fragrance that emanates from our life and the fruit those near us eat of. We all have influence—influence for good or evil, right or wrong—and with our influence we can inspire or discourage, bore or enthuse. I am sure that you have come in contact with people who by their very presence in a room produce an atmosphere of peace, joy, acceptance, or hope. They inspire you to live more generously, try harder, and rejoice more. You have also, I'm equally sure, been exposed to others whose presence fills the air with judgment, conflict, or fear. They also inspire—inspire you to leave their presence as soon as possible.

Jesus said that those of the Kingdom are to be salt that has savor—positive influence; and a light that is not hidden—helpfully revealing. Neither of these elements is neutral in their impact; they are powerful in the influence they have upon the world with which they come into contact. Jesus saw this matter of influence important enough to conclude:

> *Let your light so shine before men that they (those who see it) may see your good works (your light) and (be influenced to) glorify your Father in heaven* (Matthew 5:16, paraphrase in parentheses mine).

DESTINY

Destiny is living in, and pursuing, that for which we were designed. The writer of Hebrews stated it like this:

> *Therefore we also, since we are surrounded by so great a cloud of witnesses, let us lay aside every weight, and the sin which so easily ensnares us, and let us run with endurance the race that is set before us* (Hebrews 12:1).

For Paul, part of his race was to live in his calling (destiny) as an apostle. Living as an apostle, he was being what he was destined to be.

We all have a divine destiny to be the carriers of the Kingdom of God; it is what we were designed to be. As we live in this world pursuing this assignment, we are fulfilling our destiny as children of God. In so doing, one day we will declare with Paul, *"I have fought the good fight, I have finished the race, I have kept the faith"* (2 Tim. 4:7).

LEGACY

Legacy is that which is passed from generation to generation. It is what we place in the hands of those who follow us. If the legacy is good, it is a platform on which the next generation begins its quest for their destiny. But if it is poor, it is like a ball and chain around their legs and must be cut off in order for destiny to be pursued. The legacy we leave behind is our choice, as is our life message.

The life message we choose helps set the course for the influence our life will have, the way in which we will fulfill our destiny and the quality of the legacy we leave behind.

JEHORAM

Let me illustrate this with the contrasting lives of two men, one from Scripture and one from my life.

At the age of 32, Jehoram became king of Judah. If I could put his life message in a sentence it would best be stated as the opposite of Joshua's: *"As for me and my house, we will serve myself and not God."* Jehoram was the son of Jehoshaphat and the grandson of Asa, both great kings who trusted in the Lord. He was, however, unlike either of them.

Jehoram began his reign by killing all his brothers so that he would have no opposition to the throne, and would acquire the wealth that his father had given them. He then led the people of Judah into idol worship. In response to Jehoram's sin, God sent the prophet Elijah with a message that Jehoram would become sick with a dreadful disease of the intestines. He died a painful death after reigning only eight years. The consequences of his actions were not only felt by him personally but also by the people he ruled. Their enemies invaded the land taking its wealth, and a great plague came upon all the people.

The story of Jehoram's life and rule can be found in Second Chronicles 21. The final verses of this chapter contain three revealing statements that summarize the course Jehoram's life message set. I am taking the liberty of taking them out of order for the purpose of emphasis.

The first statement exposes the measure of Jehoram's influence: "*His people made no burning for him like the burning for his fathers*" (2 Chron. 21:19). The burning referred to the pile of incense and fragrant spices that was burned at the funeral of the king. It represented the positive influence the king had on the nation during his life. The larger the pile, the greater his influence had been in the land. Jehoram's father Jehoshaphat had been given a "great" burning because of all the good he did during his time as king. In Jehoram's case, however, the people so despised his influence that they made absolutely no burning at all.

The second statement reveals the failure of Jehoram to fulfill his destiny: "*They buried him in the City of David, but not in the tombs of the kings*" (2 Chron. 21:20).

This man was born into royalty, destined by blood to be a king. He was responsible for ensuring the well-being of the people and establishing rule that promoted the welfare and expansion of the kingdom. This was what he was made for, yet Jehoram's reign was so far from his destiny that the people thought it a farce to bury him with the true kings of their history.

This third testimonial declares the contempt that the people held for the legacy Jehoram left behind: "*He reigned in Jerusalem eight years, and **to no one's sorrow**, departed*" (2 Chron. 21:20, emphasis mine). This phrase is literally translated "departed without being desired." No one cared that he was gone; no one wished that he had not died. Jehoram's grandfather and father were men of powerful Godly influence who walked in their destiny and handed him a great legacy, yet his legacy was that he was totally forgettable.

What is not written in his biography, yet was included in the life story of other kings, is as fitting a eulogy as what is. In most of the records of the kings, there is a reference to the location of the other writings detailing the life of the king. Its absence here screams of the inferiority of Jehoram's life message and the lack of value of his influence, destiny, and legacy. His life was so lacking of contribution to the health of the nation that no one wrote further of his deeds. No one wanted to leave a greater record of all he had done for others to find.

This was a man born in privilege, given nearly unlimited possibilities to influence a generation for good, empowered to fulfill his destiny and the destiny of a nation, and offered the opportunity to pass on a legacy of greatness; yet, he made a contribution that no one wanted to remember. This is where his life message led him.

LEONARD SHIRREL

I first met Leonard Shirrel when I was about nine years old and he was in his late thirties. Leonard didn't attract my attention, but his youngest daughter did pique my interest, even at that young age. Deborah continues to interest me after 38 years of marriage.

Leonard's life message and resulting contribution stand in stark contrast to Jehoram's.

Leonard began life with little privilege and limited possibilities. He was the son of a poor farmer and his Cherokee wife, living in the hills of Oklahoma. He grew up fishing and hunting, and at the age of 16, Leonard fell from a tree and injured his hip. The injury led to a life-long limp that was so extreme his left hand nearly dragged on the ground with every other step.

He left school after the sixth grade and eventually made his way to California, where he met Connie, a 15-year-old Italian girl whose mother had died when she was an infant, and who was deserted by her father when she was 12. Leonard and Connie married less than a week after they met.

They lived most of their married life in Moss Landing, a small fishing village on the Monterey Bay, and raised two adopted daughters, Janice and Deborah. Together, Leonard and Connie owned and operated a successful commercial fishing chandlery and were married for over 40 years until Connie's death at the age of 56. Five years later—to everyone's sorrow—Leonard unexpectedly and suddenly departed.

His people—family and friends—made a "great burning" to honor his influence.

Leonard's funeral was attended by an eclectic group of people, illustrating the wide-range of influence he had during his lifetime. Included in those gathered to pay honor to my father-in-law were those from every economic and social background—doctors, fishermen, lawyers, judges, business people, and pastors. Young and old wept at their loss and laughed through their tears as humorous anecdotes were shared. All of them had been impacted by Leonard's life.

Among the group of mourners sitting in the church and later standing at his graveside were young men who owed their lives and success in life to Leonard's kindness and generosity.

Also in attendance were those whose life in Christ could be traced to the witness Leonard's life demonstrated. All who were there that day were living testimonies of the quality of Leonard's life message and the value of his influence, his destiny, and the legacy he left behind.

A Daughter's Tribute

At the time of Leonard's death, Deborah and I were living in Vacaville, about two hours from her father's home. Leonard had been admitted to the hospital for an angioplasty that the doctors declared successful. On the morning he was to go home, he dressed and waited for the doctor to give him his release. The nurse came into the room and told him it would be a few minutes longer. When she left the room, Leonard lay down on the bed to wait, and in a moment a massive blood clot hit his lung and he quietly slipped out of this life.

That same morning, Deborah called the hospital to tell her father "good morning" and was devastated when a nurse told her that her father was dead. Deb's dad was her hero, and the news left her reeling with sorrow and the disappointment that she had not been able to say goodbye. Once we got the family to Moss Landing, we made arrangements with the mortuary in Monterey for Deborah to see her father's body, a reunion that was delayed due to an autopsy to determine exact cause of death. When we arrived at the mortuary, it was late in the evening and we were escorted into a private room where Leonard's body lay on a gurney.

We mostly stood in silence as Deb laid her hand on her father's chest, and lightly caressed the face of the man who had chosen her as his daughter, taught her how to shoot a gun and catch a fish, and helped her see life as an adventure.

When Deb spoke, she longingly expressed that she wanted to take him home. He was gone, she knew that, but the physical shell in which she had so often found strength and comfort lay before her. Then, not caring if it was proper, Deborah wrapped her arms around her father's once-strong body, placing her face on his massive chest and held him with a daughter's loving warm embrace, her tears wetting the shirt in which his body was wrapped.

Several minutes later, she reluctantly released him and we left the mortuary and traveled back to her father's house in Moss Landing, with Deb again lamenting that we could not take him with us.

Would She Hold Me?

Sleep would not come to me that night; the scene of Deb's embrace had left a deep mark on my mind and emotions, and several questions troubled me. What kind of man would evoke such a response? Was it possible that one could live in a manner that even his lifeless body would hold this kind of attraction? In light of what I had witnessed, how would my life measure up when my body lay in the mortuary prepared for burial? The most troubling question was this: Would Deb hold me when I died?

Before that night was over, these questions found their way onto paper in prose that I gave to Deborah in the morning. I offer it here as a burning to a life message worth writing about, and a man whose contribution left the world a better place and our lives deeply enriched.

Will You Hold Me When I Die?

Will you hold me when I die?

When this life for me is over and your vow to me complete, will the touch we shared together draw you to me?

Will your love for me outweigh the disapproval of those who will think you silly or too emotional? Will you lay your head upon my chest, your soft sweet hair draped under my chin?

Will you hold me when I die?

When my arms can no longer comfort you, and I can give you nothing in return for your embrace, will you hesitate to leave my side and wish to take me home?

It would seem that there are greater expressions to applaud the living of two lives together, yet at this moment I can think of nothing more rewarding than to know that you will hold me when I die.

Will you hold me when I die?

Dear Lord, I need you. For without you I cannot be the man worthy of the woman you have given me. Teach me to love better, to give more, to tell her often of her priceless value. Help me Lord Jesus, so that when you call me into your arms my precious Deborah will want to hold me in hers.

Deborah—will you hold me when I die?

Written July 13, 1994, at 4:00 A.M.

CHAPTER FOUR

Who Do You Think You Are?

"Let us remember that within us there is a palace of immense magnificence."—Teresa of Avila

*H*ave you ever stopped to think about what you're thinking about?

Out of all the things that are filed away in the folders of your mind, what thoughts force their way to the surface of your thinking processes? What subject matter dominates your thinking, and what is the content of those thoughts?

I am convinced that the two most important things you think about are God and you. What you think about God and what you think about yourself creates the lens through which you see life and molds the message that flows out of your life.

This truth is illustrated in the story of Moses when he sent the spies into the Promised Land. They were to covertly sneak into the enemies' territory to scope out the land on the other side of the river and then bring back a report on what they saw.

Ten of the spies returned with a pessimistic report that reflected their own negative view of themselves: *"We seemed like grasshoppers in our own eyes"* (Num. 13:33 NIV). They were still held captive by a slave mentality and could not see that they were the chosen people of God and nothing could stand in the way of the divine purpose.

A few verses later, in the next chapter, we discover their thoughts about the God that delivered them from slavery.

> *Why has the LORD brought us to this land to fall by the sword, that our wives and children should become victims? Would it not be better for us to return to Egypt?* (Numbers 14:3)

Not only did they have a low view of themselves, they misinterpreted God's purposes and questioned His love.

Forty years later, in a retelling of the story, Moses described their flawed view of God with these words: *"You complained in your tents and said, 'Because the lord hates us, he has brought us out of the land of Egypt to deliver us into the hand of the Amorites, to destroy us'"* (Deut. 1:27).

They viewed God as hateful, deceptive, and in hostility against them. In like manner, they viewed themselves as helpless and insignificant. These two destructive beliefs helped fashion an evaluation of the situation resulting in a message of defeat and retreat. *"We are not able to go up against the people...let's select a leader and return to Egypt"* (Numbers 13:31; 14:4).

Unfortunately, their distorted image of God and inaccurate view of themselves convinced a whole nation to abandon God's plan—a plan that would establish them as

His representative nation in the world. Now, they will have 40 years in the wilderness to think about what they think about—to reconsider and reflect on the negative results of their faulty thinking and destructive words.

Caleb and Joshua stand in stark contrast to the other ten men. Caleb came back from the spying mission with this insight into how he saw himself, *"Let us go up at once and take possession, for we are well able to overcome it"* (Num. 13:30).

The next day Caleb and Joshua would stand together and make a brief statement that reveals what they thought about God: "The Lord is with us." In contrast to the other spies, Joshua and Caleb thought of God as for them, not against them, and saw themselves as capable of the task, as long as the Lord was with them. They had an exalted view of the God they served and His commitment to them as a people.

Because of their firm belief in the passion and purpose of God they were filled with courage and commitment. Even though it did not convince the nation, it pleased the heart of God and their lives were preserved so that they could go into the Promised Land.

THE ENEMY ATTACKS OUR THOUGHTS

It should be no surprise that these two areas of thought— who we are and who God is—are the main targets of the enemy as he tries to limit or destroy your life message. This assault on the human mind and thoughts started in the beginning of time in that ancient garden as the enemy focused his attention on Eve.

The point of attack against the crown of God's creation was Eve's concept of God. He was certain that if he could introduce a sliver of skepticism, he could bring her down. His cunning action began with a question designed to introduce questions about God's word. *"Has God indeed said?"* (Gen. 3:1). If she questions His word, she will question His integrity and His intentions.

He then follows up with a direct contradiction to what God had told Eve.

> *You will not surely die, for God knows that in the day you eat of it (the fruit of the tree of the knowledge of good and evil) your eyes will be opened, and you will be like God, knowing good and evil* (Genesis 3:4-5).

What was his plan? His aim was to cause Eve to believe that God was keeping things from her that would be good for her, to have her think of Him as selfish and deceptive.

As her thinking changed about God, her thinking changed about herself. How could she come to this conclusion? She had been made in the image of God, created as the perfect mate for her husband, and placed in a home that supplied everything she needed. She is confident, secure, content, and in perfect harmony with her surroundings.

With the serpent's question now ringing in her ear, darkness begins to cloud her thinking. Now, having conformed her thinking to the mental image created by the serpent, she now sees herself as needy, lacking wisdom, discontent with her present situation, and willing to choose the creation over her creator.

> *So when the woman saw that the tree was good for food, that it was pleasant to the eyes, and a tree desirable to make one wise, she took of its fruit and ate* (Genesis 3:6).

The tragic result of Eve's faulty concept of God and evaluation of herself was that she and Adam lost their innocence and became afraid of their creator.

> *Then the lord God called to Adam and said to him, "Where are you?" So he said, "I heard your voice in the garden, and I was afraid because I was naked; and I hid myself"* (Genesis 3:9,10).

The wings had been stripped from the butterfly.

THE POWER OF A THOUGHT

Paul helps us see the power of the way we think in his letter to the Roman church. He writes, *"Do not be conformed to this world but be transformed by the renewing of the mind"* (Rom. 12:2). There are several words in this verse that help us understand the meaning of Paul's concern.

The first key word is *conformed*. It means to be shaped or molded and to be conformed to a pattern. A good example is the conforming of the clay to a desired shape by the potter's hands while it is on the spinning wheel.

The next key word in this text is *transformed*. This word comes from a Greek word where we get the word "metamorphosis." It means to be made into something new, to change into another form. Metamorphosis is the word used to describe the process of a caterpillar becoming a butterfly. A curious thing about this word is that once you have been transformed, you can't go back to what you were. I've never heard of a butterfly becoming a caterpillar. The metamorphosis can only go in one direction.

A third word worth noting is the word *renewing* which simply means a renovation or rewiring of something, such as a house that has gone through an extreme makeover. Thayer's Lexicon states that it is a "complete change for the better." It implies a shift that makes our thinking better.

The last word we will look at is the word *mind*. This word has to do with the way we think, our mind-sets and mental posture. It is like a computer that stores our thoughts and is characterized by the private conversations we have with ourselves.

Assembling all these truths together, we come to the impact of Paul's passion as he writes these words. Paul is telling us not to allow our lives to be shaped into the image or character of this world, or be conformed to the way the world thinks, but be made into something new by a complete renovation or rewiring of the way we think.

Paul is confirming the dynamic power of the mind. Our very being can be transformed when the way we think is renewed, renovated, being completely changed for the better. This is what repentance is, changing the way we think, and it is accomplished when we come into agreement with the Holy Spirit as He brings us revealed truth.

How we think about God and how we think about ourselves are in some ways two sides to the same coin. The way we think about God affects the way we think about ourselves and the way we think about ourselves influences the way we think about God. It is nearly impossible to talk about the one without bringing up the other.

The Voices in Our Thoughts

Let's focus on our thoughts about ourselves. I believe that the thoughts we have about ourselves will dramatically impact how we see God.

So, who do you think you are? In your quietest moments what are your thoughts about yourself?

The curious thing about the mind is that there is more than just your voice speaking. There are several voices that influence how we see ourselves. One of those is our physical and emotional environment. Our thoughts are powerfully influenced by the way we were raised, the culture we grew up in, the function or dysfunction of our family, our religious upbringing, and our ethnic and national cultures.

It is no wonder Gideon was found hiding in a winepress believing he was of the weakest clan of his tribe and he was the least in his father's house.

How was he to believe that he was the mighty man of valor the angel declared him to be when for the last seven years his nation had been hiding in caves from an enemy that would raid their crops and steal their flocks? His physical and emotional environment helped shape a negative image of himself.

Another influence on how we think about ourselves is the judgment pronounced by the significant people in our lives. If we are told often enough that we are smart or valuable we will soon begin to believe it. Those words have the power to make us believe in ourselves. If the people around you believe you can do anything, you begin to believe it too. The opposite is also true. If our heads have been filled with negative words like, *you are stupid* or, *you will never amount to anything*, then we attach ourselves to those words and become their prisoners.

When I was in the second grade the teacher gave us an assignment to draw a picture of a farm animal. I chose to draw a horse. Each student was then asked to present our drawing to the class. I believe that her objective was to inspire us to greater creativity. Unfortunately, I did not experience that inspiration and creativity she was aiming for.

When I stood before the class and showed them my horse, my fellow classmates were puzzled. Seeing how puzzled they were, I told them it was a horse. Rather then getting praise, I got ridiculed. They laughed and said it looked more like a cow than a horse.

I stood there in silence becoming more and more humiliated. It was many years later that I realized that I had adopted their judgment and came to think of myself as being empty of any creativity.

Who Are You?

Someone once said that the most important opinion you have is the one you have of yourself, and the most significant things you say all day are those things you say to yourself. Those opinions that we have of ourselves are often influenced by the way we evaluate our failures or successes. These judgments we make about what we have done can be very loud voices of influence.

When Moses left Egypt, after killing the Egyptian, he lived in the backside of the desert spending forty years reflecting on his failure in Egypt. By doing so he allowed that failure to be the measure of who he was, and when a God opportunity knocked on his door his response was, "*Who am I that I should go to Pharaoh and that I should bring the children of Israel out of Egypt?*" (Exod. 3:11).

There are many things that influence the way we think about ourselves. However, there is only one voice that is more important than any other voice that rings in our ears. This voice is one hundred percent accurate and is the only one opinion that can be trusted—it is the voice of the Father.

Any personal identity rooted outside of who God declares us to be will be distorted at best. This does not exclude the importance of the need for accountability and influence among trusted friends and family. However, if we allow other appraisals to be the determining factor in the way we think about ourselves we will be subjected to man's faulty opinion, held captive to our culture and history, and find ourselves with an inferior life message.

THE PRODIGAL SON

This classic story and most famous of the Jesus stories begins with the youngest son asking for his inheritance. What you may not have noticed when reading this story is that the father distributes the inheritance to both his sons, not just the youngest.

> *And the younger of them said to his father, 'Father, give me the portion of goods that falls to me.'* **So he divided to them his livelihood** (Luke 15:12, emphasis added).

This is important to note, as you will see later. The oldest son chooses to stay with his father while the youngest takes off to another country, losing everything in wasteful living. He then returns, hoping to find a place of employment among his father's servants. Instead he is welcomed as a son and celebrated for his return.

Traditionally, when we look at this story the focus is exclusively on the younger son. Permit me to bypass that portion of the story. Let's go to the end of the story and center our thoughts on the older son. In the conversation between the father and the older son we will also find a critical truth.

As we zero-in on the verbal exchange between father and son, the heart of the older son is revealed. His words reflect a completely inaccurate idea of who he is. It is clear that he fails to accept the appraisal of his father.

Here is what the father has to say about his son, *"And he said to him, 'Son, you are always with me, and all that I have is yours'"* (Luke 15:31). Let's break it down into three important declarations of the father.

Son—This is the young man's true identity. He is not a servant, a slave, or even a hired hand. He is the son of his father. Any other view is a defective view.

You are always with me—the father is telling his son that he has a place in his heart that no other can have. This is his access to a place of intimacy with the father. He is a son of honor that has a place in the presence of the father that no other person could demand.

All that I have is yours—this is the father's declaration of both his son's inheritance and favor. Because you are my son you not only have a favored place, you have favored privileges.

The true identity of the elder son, as declared by the father, is that he is a beloved son with intimate access to his father with all inheritance rights and privileges. Here is the sad part of the story. The son never thought of himself in that way. Because of his inaccurate view of himself, he had an inaccurate view of the father. Because of those inaccuracies, he was jealous of his brother and angry with his father. Listen to his words:

> *Lo, these many years I have been serving you; I never transgressed your commandment at any time; and yet you*

*never gave me a young goat that I might make merry
with my friends. But as soon as this son of yours came,
who has devoured your livelihood with harlots; you killed
the fatted calf for him* (Luke 15:29,30).

Notice first that this son had a religious relationship with
his father rather than a loving, intimate, co-operative one. A
religious relationship is one where the greatest value is placed
on what we do *for* each other and strict compliance with the
"rules." His relationship with his father was based on *what he
did* rather than *who he was.*

An incorrect image of ourselves will lead us into centering
our focus on working *for* God rather than focusing on living
in intimate fellowship and co-laboring *with* God. Those who
work for God live like hirelings, working for wages. They
expect a paycheck. However, those that properly understand
their relationship with God know they are sons that co-labor
with the Father in expanding the family business and live
out of their inheritance.

This son measured his life by his obedience to the rules,
rather than the quality of his relationship with his father. He
didn't know who he was, so his identity came from what he
did, rather than from being his father's son.

It is interesting how the older son's views sank into the
darkness of self-pity and limited possibilities: *"You never gave
me a young goat that I may make merry with my friends"* (Luke
15:29). Can you imagine what his father must have been
thinking? "Everything I have is yours and this is your life's
dream? To have a goat so you can party with your friends—is
that all you expect out of life? What are you thinking?"

You can only dream as big as your identity will allow
you. Who you think you are will set the boundaries of
your life message. Maxwell Maltz, an American surgeon

and motivational speaker, put it this way. *Self-image sets the boundaries of individual accomplishment.*

If you believe you are a slave in the kingdom you will never see beyond your present need. However, if you know you are a son in your father's kingdom you can set your sights on what your imagination sees.

Notice lastly that the elder brother's twisted view of himself left him with no sense of family. He wouldn't even call his father's son his brother; he spitefully called him *"This son of yours."* He couldn't enter into his father's joy or celebrate his brother's redemption.

What should have been a joyous family reunion was downsized to a judgment against his brother and his father. The measure of his own life—obedience to the rules—became the measure by which he passed judgment on others.

It is a tragic thing to have a loving father and yet have all the classic characteristics of an orphan—self-absorbed, lack of true identity, insecure, difficulty in bonding, fear of intimacy, and an abiding anger. This is a good description of this man's life message, formed in part by who he believed he was. It makes me wonder who the real prodigal is in this story. Both brothers wasted their inheritance, one through intentional debauchery and the other through neglect.

What are you thinking about? The father of these two prodigals represents the character and nature of our heavenly Father, and here is what He thinks about you: *"Son, Daughter, you are always with me, and everything I have belongs to you."*

Who do you think you are? Will your answer be in balance with what God thinks about you? Your answer may determine more than you realize.

CHAPTER FIVE

Finding Your Voice

"Freedom is knowing who you really are."
—Linda Thomson

*W*e have been called—invited—to have an em-powered destiny and a life-giving voice in our world. Until we embrace the person God says we are, our destiny remains a longing and our voice an echo. The power of our life message is stuck in our history if we ignore the invitation God has extended to us to step into our true identity. I speak from personal experience.

Before I tell you of this experience, let me share some insights from a familiar story. It is the story of Zacharias, found in the first chapter of the Book of Luke. I suggest you take the time now to read the passage before you continue with this chapter, since I will be weaving my story with his.

Finished? Good, now we can continue.

How would you like to be given a prophetic word that you were going to be the father of a man who would call a nation to repentance, turn the hearts of fathers to their children, be known by God as a great man, be filled with the Holy Spirit while in his mother's womb, and have the spirit and power of one of the greatest prophets in the Bible?

Then add to the magnitude of the prophecy the fact that you and your wife are too old to have children and your wife has always been barren. Would you find the word hard to believe?

Well, Zacharias found this prophetic declaration from Gabriel so difficult to believe that he mocked the word with a "you've got to be kidding" response: *"How shall I know this? For I am an old man, and my wife is well advanced in years"* (Luke 1:18). This was not an innocent inquiry but a blatant statement of unbelief. "How shall I know this?" could legitimately be translated, "You will never convince me of this."

I Don't Want to Hear It

The first time I heard a prophet tell me I had an apostolic call on my life, it was a rather strange experience. Deborah and I were visiting the evening worship service at Bethel Church in Redding, California. During the ministry time at the end of the preaching, we were speaking with our then new friend, Kris Vallotton. He was sharing something with Deb when he turned to me and made a pointed declaration that went something like this, "You have an apostolic call but you don't want to hear it." He then returned to his conversation with Deb and I was left to contemplate his words.

He was right; I didn't want to hear it because I couldn't see it and if you can't see it you can't become it.

It would take a few years and much encouragement by friends before I began to accept the truth of the call and attempt to live as if I believed it.

Graham Cooke recently called this "practicing your persona." He described persona as "the way you're known in heaven."

The practice has been good for me and has been a great learning experience with God consistently confirming my call. But there is a difference between accepting God's appraisal and stepping fully into it. It was only recently that I came to understand this and saw what I couldn't see before. Thanks to the ministry of close friends, a huge shift came in the way I think about myself, and this in turn has released a greater apostolic anointing and authority. The shift came as God used a past failure to reveal His perspective of who I am. Let's first go back to Zacharias' story.

IDENTITY CHANGE

Gabriel was changing Zacharias' identity from a sonless priest to the father of the man who would make the final preparation for the coming of the Messiah. He must have anticipated that this was going to be an easy sell. Zacharias would have been raised on the story of Abraham becoming the father of a nation through the miraculous conception and birth of Isaac.

As a priest, he would have confessed his belief in the God of the miraculous, and he knew the prophecies about the One who would come and prepare the way of the Messiah. If that wasn't enough to give Gabriel confidence in his reception, the announcement he was to deliver was a direct answer to Zacharias' own prayer!

No wonder Gabriel was a bit miffed at Zacharias' failure to embrace the word. You can hear the consternation in his words:

> *I am Gabriel, who stands in the presence of God, and was sent to speak to you and bring you these glad tidings **(you jerk!)**. But behold, you will be mute and not able to speak until the day these things take place **because you did not believe my words which will be fulfilled in their own time*** (Luke 1:19-20, emphasis and additions added).

Zacharias' refusal to accept his new identity cost him his voice.

One's voice is more than the making of sound. Our voice is a creative force speaking into being what previously did not exist. It is a part of our authority and influence. When we lose our voice, we lose the power of our message. Zacharias lost his prophetic voice because of his unbelief and his unwillingness to come into agreement with the way Heaven viewed him—the father of the Messiah's forerunner, John.

SEEING FROM A NEW PERSPECTIVE

At the age of 19, I was hit by a drunk driver while riding a motorcycle. My leg was badly broken and the femur had to be pieced back together with screws and a stainless steel rod placed down through the marrow of the bone. The rod was intended to be a temporary way of stabilizing the leg, allowing it to heal. After several weeks in the hospital, I was released and walked with the help of crutches.

Several weeks later, still walking with crutches, I was visiting my sister with Deborah, my then fiancée. A cousin of mine was also at the house, and he had his large motorcycle with him. I don't know if it was wanting to get back on the horse that threw me or just simple stupidity, but I climbed onto the cycle against Deborah's plea not to.

I sat on the bike and when I shifted my weight, my foot kicked the kickstand and the bike began to fall. I tried to hold the bike, but it fell and my broken leg took the weight of it, bending the steel rod.

The result of this foolish action was that my leg eventually healed in that bent position, leaving the leg shorter than the other, and I was forced to live with a measure of constant pain. I also walk with a limp. What I didn't know for 35 years was that I was living with a subtle sense of shame over my failure to act wisely. I also didn't realize that I was walking with a limp in my calling and destiny, limiting the authority of my apostolic voice. Recently, the Lord used the motorcycle experience to awaken me to both realities.

This year I was with our students in the Philippines. The students were insistent on praying for my leg, and there was a great level of faith to see it healed. None of them knew the cause of the problem, so I was surprised when one of the students told me he was hearing one word as he was praying for me. That word was "kickstand."

Well, that elevated my faith, and I asked Bill and Carol Dew, members of our team from The Mission who have a great anointing for healing, to pray for me.

After a time of prayer, Carol asked me what I was feeling and was surprised when I said, "Shame." I, too, was surprised.

Carol asked if I wanted to take care of it, and I enthusiastically agreed. The three of us went to their hotel room and we prayed through some important issues of shame and feelings of inadequacy. I left their room with a great sense of peace. I went back to my room and quickly fell asleep. Sometime in the middle of the night, I awoke praying and processing the evening's events. I asked the Lord if He would take me back to that moment 35 years ago and help me see it the way He did.

Identity Upgrade

I didn't have a vision but I knew I was in that same place again, this time with Jesus. I didn't have the shame that was with me the evening before, but I waited to hear what the Lord had to say. He said, "Though your actions that night were unwise, a motorcycle can't move forward until the kickstand is released and I have made you to kick over kickstands so the bike can move forward." My life message took a major upgrade in that moment.

Those words opened a door to my persona that I immediately chose to walk through and a new confidence to embrace who He says I am. The Lord broke the identity that shame had held me in and released me to my destiny. He freed me to say "yes" to my call. Though I still limp physically, I am now learning to walk in my call without a limp and to speak with a new voice.

One of the things I find interesting about the story of Zacharias is that he did not get his voice back when the baby was born, but when he obediently broke tradition and named the boy John. In naming him John, he was declaring that this son was unlike any other in their family history—a man of a different spirit. He was making a statement, not only of his son's identity, but of his own: "I am the father of John." When he did, he regained his voice.

A New Voice, a New Man

Now the exciting part for me is this: When Zacharias got his voice back, he went from being a deaf, mute, unbelieving priest to a man stepping into his destiny as the concluding voice in the great line of prophets who prophesied the coming of the Messiah, like David, Micah, Isaiah, Daniel (see Luke 1:62). They all said, "The time is coming," but Zacharias was given the voice to declare, "The time is now."

> *Blessed is the Lord God of Israel, for He has visited and redeemed His people, and **has** raised up a horn of salvation for us in the house of his servant David* (Luke 1:68-69, emphasis added).

By embracing his heavenly persona, Zacharias was also given the voice to prophesy into his son's destiny and then guide him to its fulfillment:

> *And you, child, will be called the prophet of the Highest; For you will go before the face of the Lord to prepare His ways* (Luke 1:76).

Jump ahead with me 30 years and listen as we hear the resonance of Zacharias' prophecy in John's declaration:

I am "The voice of one crying in the wilderness: Make straight the way of the Lord" (John 1:23).

Zacharias found his voice when he believed, declared, and acted on the proclamation of his heavenly identity.

My life message, like Zacharias' and yours, is not static; it is a living thing that will continue to grow as long as we live, and if in agreement with Heaven, it will have an eternal impact on the generations to come. I am living with a brilliant anticipation of what will be added in the years ahead.

CHAPTER SIX

Divine Contradictions

"Every saint has a past, and every sinner has a future."—Oscar Wilde

"With a past like mine, how can I ever have a life that can be respected and helpful?"

"How can I have a positive life message, coming from the dysfunctional family and culture I was raised in?"

I have heard these statements or similar expressions a hundred times or more over my years in vocational ministry. They come from people who have become convinced that their past determines their future, that the hurtful, cruel words spoken to them by significant people in their lives are predictions of their potential. They have come to believe a lie—one propagated by the enemy in order to keep them stuck in their history and unable to live their God-intended purpose.

The truth is that God loves to contradict the predictions of our upbringing, our failures and the labels put on us by others. The Bible is full of those who began in failure but rose to triumph, those whose background would disqualify them from greatness, only to surprise all as they fulfilled a powerful destiny.

BELOVED CONTRADICTIONS

Take, for instance, Peter, a man who denied his relationship with Jesus only to become one of the most influential men in the early church. What about the woman at the well, living with a man who was not her husband, having had five of them, yet her life message is that her testimony, *"Come, see a Man who told me all things that I ever did. Could this be the Christ?"* brought a village to believe in Jesus (John 4:29-30)? How about Paul, one who took great pride in persecuting the Christians, yet became the most prolific writer of the New Testament? Part of his life message is expressed in his own writing:

> *Therefore, if anyone is in Christ, he is a new creation; old things have passed away; behold, all things have become new* (2 Corinthians 5:17).

We all have heard of Jabez, thanks to the great book, *The Prayer of Jabez*, by Bruce Wilkinson. Jabez's story is tucked away in the genealogies of First Chronicles, chapter four. There is no reference to his parents' names. His birth was so painful that his mother gave him a name that labeled him for the rest of his life: *Jabez*, meaning "one who causes pain." Every time he heard his name, he would have been reminded of what his mother thought of him, blamed for something he had no choice in. He was tagged with a name that predicted his life message—one who causes pain.

But remember—Father loves to contradict the predictions of our past. In spite of Jabez's painful beginning and his mother's prediction, the writer of the Bible, the Holy Spirit, thought so much of Jabez's life message that He interrupted the genealogies in order to record it and tell his story:

> *Now Jabez was more honorable than his brothers....And Jabez called on the God of Israel saying, "Oh, that You would bless me indeed, and enlarge my territory, that Your hand would be with me, and that You would keep me from evil, that I may not cause pain!" So God granted him what he requested* (1 Chronicles 4:9-10).

He started by causing pain, yet became a man whose life message was that he was more honorable than his brothers, a man of great favor and influence, and a man who *did not* cause pain. His life message contradicted his beginnings.

MY WIFE

Jabez's story reminds me of a woman I have known since I was a young boy—my wife, Deborah.

My wife is probably one of the most remarkable women in the world. She is a fantastic wife, a great mother, and a wonderful and loved grandmother. She is astonishingly creative, intelligent, and fun. When she steps up to the platform to share a thought from the Holy Spirit, everyone pays attention and all are rewarded with life-transforming insights and revelations. Deborah walks in great favor and declares a message that radiates the goodness of God.

The circumstances around Deborah's conception did not predict the life I just described. In fact, in our present social climate she would have most likely been aborted.

She was the result of a rape of a 12-year-old girl by an extended family member. To this young girl, the fetus in her womb was an unwanted child that would constantly remind her and her family of a tragic and brutal event. But the Father loves to contradict the predictions of our beginnings. Deborah was adopted into a loving family on the day of her birth and grew to be the woman we now enjoy. Her conception has not dictated her destiny or her life message.

My Dad

Allow me to tell you two more who are personal to me. They are the stories of Wesley and Helen Crone, my parents.

My father is one of the heroes in my life. In fact, to me he is one of the great men of the Kingdom. He has walked with God for over 60 years, been faithful to the same woman for the same length of time, provided for his family, and has established a legacy of integrity, perseverance, and honor.

His positive life message has been an encouragement and inspiration not only to his two children, but to the countless young men he has counseled over the years. I do not believe it is an exaggeration to state that my father has the respect of everyone who has ever known him—especially mine.

Now, here is the rest of the story—or more accurately— the beginnings of Dad's life message.

My father was raised during the Great Depression, a most difficult time in America. To say they were poor is inadequate to describe their financial condition. Though my grandfather worked, they never had enough to support their four children. Dad remembers living often in the parks or out in the forest in tents. They often had to relocate. One day, Dad came home to find that his family had moved while he was in school and he had to find them.

I took my father to see the movie *The Cinderella Man*, a story set in the Great Depression. I thought that he would enjoy it as an inspiring account of someone overcoming great odds. However, when I asked my dad what he thought of it, he softly expressed that the movie was difficult to watch because it reminded him of too many painful memories.

My dad's social and financial conditions, growing up in the Depression, were not the worst of his childhood. To say that my grandparents were dysfunctional is almost a compliment compared to the reality. They were angry, jealous, and hurt people, and as we know, hurt people *hurt people*.

My father was born into the family when my grandfather was in his forties, and he became the whipping boy of the family. Though I never heard Dad speak of physical abuse, verbal and emotional abuse was certainly rampant.

Dad has never spoken much of his childhood, but recently I got a greater glimpse into it when I told him I was writing this book and wanted to include his story. He said, "I cannot remember any pleasant memories from my childhood. All of my memories are of hearing yelling and seeing the dishes fly across the room." He then brightened and said, "The only good memory I have is of my oldest sister wheeling me in a wagon. She was the one who changed my diapers and took care of me."

Living in a culture of lack, anger, abuse, and dysfunction, my father had little chance to have a positive life message. But God contradicted the predictions of his past and gave him a message of hope, blessing, and healing.

My Mother

My mother, though opposite to my father in personality, is equal in her character, influence, and place in the Kingdom. There are women around the globe who have been impacted through my mom's teaching and example. She gave her life to Christ as a young girl and has never looked back, living as an authentic Christian woman. She has prayed many family members into the Kingdom. My mom's life message, like my father's, has left a mark on all with whom she has come in contact. She has a place in my heart like no other.

Mom, too, has more to her story:

She was born into a family of nine children. Her mother was a powerful woman of faith, but her father was an excessively angry man described by my grandmother as being "so mean he didn't need alcohol to make him cruel." What little contact his children had with him was filled with fear and intimidation. If it were not for the generosity of my grandmother's brother, the family would not have survived. He provided a house, most would call a shack, for the family on the backside of his farm in southern Idaho and made sure they didn't starve. I personally have fond memories of "Uncle Bob" and no memories of my grandfather, as I never met him.

It was only a few years ago that mom's brother, Wallace, revealed a story of his father that he had kept hidden since he was a young boy. This story illustrates the family atmosphere created by my grandfather. One day, his dad told Wallace to get into the truck, and they drove down the road. After a short trip, my grandfather stopped the truck and got out, instructing my uncle to stay in the vehicle. He then walked down the road, around the corner, and stood in front of a farmhouse. What he didn't realize was that Wallace had followed and was standing behind him.

Grandfather yelled out a greeting, and a man walked out onto the front porch. He asked the man if his name was so-and-so. When the man answered positively, my grandfather pulled out the pistol it was his custom to carry and fatally shot the man. He then turned to go back to his truck and spotted his son standing wide-eyed in the middle of the road. He threatened Wallace and told him to never tell anyone what he saw. My uncle had discovered what none of the family knew—his father was the hit man for the local sheepherders.

Drunkenness, intimidation, fear, anger, and violence are not the stuff that predicts a strong, healthy life message. But God loves to contradict our history, and he did just that for my mom. Her life message declares love, forgiveness, faith, and trust.

Your Decisions Are Greater Than Your History

Your history does not have to hold your life message hostage. It is not the facts of your past that determine the quality of your message, but rather the decisions that you make from this time forward. You can have a powerful life message no matter from where you start. You can do what Jabez, Deborah, and my mom and dad did—call on God and live in the promise of the Father.

Paul understood this when he wrote:

Forgetting those things that are behind and reaching forward to those things which are ahead, I press toward the goal for the prize of the upward call of God in Christ Jesus (Philippians 3:13-14).

My version reads like this:

I let my old reputation, all my failures, all my past, lay at the feet of the Cross and will not allow them to predict or determine my potential, my future, or my destiny. Instead I take hold of the destiny, potential, and future that Christ has established for me.

Chapter Seven

The Power of Language

"Words create worlds."
—Abraham Herschel

*I*t is not a new revelation to any of us that words have power. We all have experienced the sensation of the air being suddenly sucked out of a room when someone makes a statement that everyone is thinking but no one has the guts to say. On the other hand, the proverbial elephant sitting in the middle of the table during an important meeting is taken down to size when words are put to its existence.

Words have the power to build up or tear down. They create atmosphere and increase or release tension. Words strengthen determination, release courage, and unleash hope. They also can deflate resolve, create confusion, and produce discouragement. The power of the tongue is in the words it forms, and that power releases life or death.

Ideologies, concepts, strategies all find power in the language used to describe them. Before they are given language, they remain hidden and lack the ability to be transmitted. An idea partnered with language is like the two parts of a compound being joined together to form a powerful chemical reaction. The one without the other leaves them both without transforming influence.

Two Examples

The same is true of identity. In the 1930s, Germany was wallowing in debt and astronomical inflation. It required a wheelbarrow full of German Marks to buy a loaf of bread. The government did not have the answers, and the nation was without an identity. Along came a man who understood the power of language. Hitler, though evil in his intent, expressed his ideology with such powerful words that he was able to give Germany an identity that pulled the people together, gathered resources, and raised it to become one of the most powerful and feared nations in modern history. His rise to power and Germany's recovery from financial and social depression was due in part to the synergy created by the power of language.

At The Mission, we discovered the importance of language when we put into writing the decisions we had made during the years of transition. Prior to putting these decisions in written form, we would often answer the question of identity in a very vague sort of way that had little impact or influence. Though we were sure of the things that were in our heart to do and become, without language, we were lacking a definition that focused the power of what God was doing in us. Once we began to put language to our values, people began to be drawn to what was being declared, and the effectiveness of the ministry increased. By putting language to the life message of The Mission, we released a power that is transforming us as a community of believers.

One's personal life message is also given power to transform when it can be put into words and given language that encapsulates its essence. Gideon is a prime example.

GIDEON AND DAVE

For seven years, the nation of Israel had been hard-pressed under the thumb of foreign armies. Every year their crops were taken and their cattle and sheep stolen. They were living in fear and hiding in caves. Gideon had no identity other than as one who hides in a wine press winnowing his wheat. That is until the Angel of the Lord shows up and puts language to Gideon's life message: *"Gideon, 'you mighty man of valor'"* (Judg. 6:12). He then follows Gideon's victim whining with, *"Go in this might of yours and you shall save Israel from the hand of the Midianites"* (Judg. 6:14). Though it took process, giving language to Gideon's identity and life message helped transform a frightened young man hiding from his enemies into the commander of an army that would set the nation free.

Gideon's story is a bit like my own. Though I was not hiding in a wine press, I was cowering in the cave of "safe" ministry. My true identity and my desired life message were buried under the fear of failure, and my faith tied to a calculator. My life message would go something like, "Play it safe, limit your risk, and keep your dreams within possible reach."

All this changed when God began to redefine my life message. A large part of that redefinition took place when I found language that declared the message I wanted my life to proclaim. The language of NIS brought a focus and power to my way of living and ministering that is nothing short of transformational. My life has gone from doing only the possible to experiencing the above and beyond what I could ask or think.

Putting language to the message of our life helps establish an important internal accountability. A countless number of times, I have been called up to walk the high road by the voice of NIS. I call this my "no option" option.

No Options

A friend of mine, an avid handball player at the time, told me the following story over 30 years ago. I honestly don't know if the story is a real-life event or a modern-day parable, but either way, it makes an important point. A man was asked the secret to his success as a tournament handball player. The questioner was especially curious about the answer as the man had only one arm and handball is played using both hands. The man's answer was simply this: "No options."

The handball player was making the point that he never had to hesitate in order to choose which hand to use. The hesitation, however slight, of the two-handed player, he felt, put the player at a disadvantage and gave him the edge.

Shortly after our church chose to leave our denomination, I had a difficult choice to make. The process of withdrawing the church included the need for me to resign my ordination with the denomination. In order to do this, there were several procedures I was to follow, and the organization concluded that I had not followed them properly, and therefore could not resign, but would be dismissed.

At the moment of the decision by the local district, I was not too concerned and accepted their conclusion, though I did not agree with it. Then I received the official letter of dismissal from the national office and my sense of "justice" rose up in me.

I was being listed among those who had been dismissed for moral failure, misappropriation of church funds, and a variety of other "crimes." All I had done was lead the church in leaving the denomination, an act allowed by the association bylaws. The letter of dismissal offered an appeal process, and I was determined to take advantage of it.

Thoughts of how I would defend myself filled my mind several times a day and often into the night. My defense would be a masterpiece that would shame them and leave them speechless. Then one morning I awoke with a thought that I knew was from the Holy Spirit: "Staying where you are is not an option." It wasn't until several hours later that I realized that God was not giving me a sermon title—but was talking about me.

A Divine Conversation

I had one of the most direct conversations with the Father that I can ever remember. It went like this:

"Father, you're talking to me, aren't you?"

"Yes I am."

"And you're talking about me trying to defend myself aren't you?"

"Yes I am."

"And you are saying that I don't have the option of defending myself?"

"That's correct. If you want to move on to fulfill your entire destiny, staying where you are in defending yourself is not an option."

It was evident from that brief conversation that fulfilling my destiny, living from my life message, left me without an option—I had only one hand to hit the ball with. It was a hand of blessing, and not defense. By the end of that day, I had written a letter of blessing to the men of the local association, expressing my love for them, thanking them for the years of friendship and partnership in the gospel, and committing myself to abide by their decision.

I don't know what effect, if any, this letter had on these men, but I am confident of its impact on propelling me toward the greater things hidden by God in my future.

A Practical Example

A few months ago, I was in the Philippines teaching in our School of the Supernatural. I have traveled enough to know there are places in the world where you have to be very careful about what you eat or drink. The Philippines is one of those places, and I had been careful to drink and brush my teeth with only bottled water. However, when eating lunch in a restaurant one day, I ordered a blended coffee, forgetting that it consists of chopped ice.

By the time the evening came around, I was feeling quite nauseated and wanted to stay close to the toilet in my room. This was a problem because I was the one scheduled to speak that night. As I lay on my bed shaking with the chills from a low-grade fever and trying to manage the pain in my stomach, I seriously considered the offer of the other speakers to take my place. It was then that I was reminded of the "no option" option, and a resolve rose up from my spirit and expressed itself with this declaration, "There's no destiny in this bed."

I knew there was no choice; a piece of my destiny awaited me in front of those students that night and staying in that bed was not an option. After crawling out of bed, each step toward the classroom made me stronger and I was able to speak with a fresh anointing. Then at the end of the teaching, I turned the class over to my colleague, Dano, for ministry and ran from the room, just in time to make it to the porcelain throne. Destiny doesn't always look like what you expect!

DEFEATING FEAR

On another occasion, Deborah and I were invited to participate with a high-profile ministry in a format that I had never experienced before. I immediately decided to reject the invitation with the justification that I was not interested in that particular format and would therefore not be effective doing it. I began to email the ministry intending to type the following: "Thank you for your invitation to minister with you; however, I will be unable to participate."

But when I started typing the "however," I stopped, and heard my inner voice repeat words I had publicly confessed several times since pursuing my life message—"If I feel fear when faced with an opportunity, I purposely accept the opportunity in order to defeat the fear." I then knew that my decision was not based on the dislike of the format, but was a decision based on fear and anxiety over doing something I had never done before.

At that moment, the Holy Spirit reminded me that a greater anointing often hides on the other side of stretching and challenging circumstances. My finger then deleted the word "however" and I typed the phrase, "I would be happy to accept and look forward to the opportunity." NIS challenged my thinking and held me accountable to my commitment to transformation.

As a side note, Deborah and I took on the opportunity and, frankly, we didn't feel that it went very well. We were, however, excited that fear had been defeated, and we lived with the expectation that we were now walking in a new level of anointing.

Only a short time later, we saw the fulfillment of this expectation as we ministered for the first time as a couple, in a women's conference in Australia—another of those uncomfortable invitations challenged by NIS. Though this was an unfamiliar place and context, we recognized a fresh power in the release of our anointing.

Importance of Partnership

Putting language to our life message can also attract the essential element of partnership.

I love the story of Jonathan and his armor-bearer. It is a great picture of one man's understanding of not only his personal life message, but also the message and identity of his nation.

Jonathan and the army of Israel were trapped by their historical enemy, the Philistines, between a mountain on one side and a cliff on the other. Though they were pitted against a well-trained and armed enemy, none of the people of Israel had weapons except Jonathan and his father, Saul. They were being harassed, intimidated, and facing extinction.

What I love about Jonathan is his understanding that staying where they were was not an option and the situation they were in was not congruent with what he knew of their life message—that of the chosen and favored people of the God of all power. Without telling his father, he decided to go on the offensive and invited the young man who took care of his armor to partner with him in this adventure. In this moment of decision, Jonathan puts language to his life message, and in so doing comes into partnership with his armor-bearer, and more importantly, the God of Israel.

> *Come, **let us** go over to the garrison of these uncircumcised; it may be that the LORD will work **for us**. For nothing restrains the LORD from saving by many or by few* (1 Samuel 14:6, emphasis added).

There it is—the message that attracted the partnership of a young man and of Heaven. The armor-bearer's response was one of a willing companion and must have emboldened Jonathan even more: *"Do all that is in your heart. Go then; here I am with you, according to your heart"* (1 Sam. 14:7). Heaven's response was a timely earthquake, causing the enemy to fear a weaponless youngster and a man with a sword and a message.

Partnership with others and with God is an essential ingredient for us to bring our dreams into reality; this is a desired result of defining one's life message.

THE CRONE FAMILY: DREAMS COME TRUE

One of the results of adopting NIS as a way of describing the core of our life message was that we began to be internally challenged to take our dreams out of the hidden places of our heart and into our lives. We put legs to this challenge when we were on a family vacation at beautiful Lake Tahoe.

The assignment for each member of our family was to put down on paper our dreams in specific terms. Not willing to live in the inferior state of dreams unrealized, we agreed to partner together for each other's declarations. We chose to believe God's promise that if we delighted ourselves in Him, He would give us the desires of our heart. Little did we realize the power that would be released by simply putting our dreams on paper and partnering with each other and the Father to see them come true.

ARTIST AND AUTHOR

Let me tell you just a little of what happened in the next 12 months. One of Deborah's dreams was to have her paintings hanging in an art gallery on Front Street in Lahaina, Maui. This was no inferior dream, as Hawaii is considered one of the largest art selling communities in the world. On top of that, at the time of putting her dream on paper she had only been painting a few months, having never had an art lesson in her life. Within a year, her art was displayed on Front Street, she was the featured artist at one of the largest art galleries in Maui, and is also now one of the featured artist, at an art gallery in the beautiful Napa Valley.

I had two dreams that required the partnership both of friends and of Heaven. One was to write a book, and the other was to plant a School of the Supernatural in another nation.

By the end of the first year, I wrote and self-published my first book, *Decisions that Define Us,* and started a school in the Philippines. In fact, I am typing the rough draft of this chapter sitting in a hotel room in Bacolod, Philippines, waiting to start, in about two hours, the third session of the second year of The School of the Supernatural.

Birth, Business, and a "Hot Betty"

My son Ryan and his brother Jeremy dreamt of owning an Irish pub and restaurant. At the time, Jeremy was a manager for New York Life, and Ryan was the youth pastor at The Mission.

Within the year following our family vacation, Ryan started attending a culinary academy, Jeremy began his exit from New York Life, and they put into action their plan. Though there is much more to the story, I will simply tell you that they are the proud owners and operators of the very successful "Stout Brothers Irish Pub and Restaurant" in downtown Santa Rosa.

My daughter wanted a photography business and to give birth to a child. The photography business was easy; the child took a miracle. Within the year, both were well on their way.

Jason, a young man we have "adopted" into our family wanted to have a "Hot Betty," which we were informed meant a wife. Today Jason is happily married to a beautiful woman named Janeen. They have purchased their first house, and have welcomed their first child, a boy, into their family.

Seven dreams expressed, seven dreams fulfilled. As a family we are convinced that giving language to our life message gave power to our dreams and attracted the partnership we needed to see those dreams become reality. We gave language to our passion and Heaven said, "Amen."

Chapter Eight

A Loss Worth Weeping Over

*"The deeper the sorrow the less
tongue it hath."* —The Talmud

*P*salm 137 is a song that is sung like a Greek tragedy whose lyrics are tinted with words of weeping and sorrow. The song is sung by the Jewish remnant now living as captives in Babylon.

It was the time in Israel's history often referred to as 70 years of captivity. The Israelites' rebellious heart had led them to ignore the warnings of the prophet Jeremiah, and the result was the destruction of Jerusalem and the relocation of surviving children of Israel to the foreign land of Babylon.

The *Psalmist* begins his song with this lament, *"By the rivers of Babylon, there we sat down, yea, we wept when we remembered Zion"* (Ps. 137:1). Who could really blame them for their sorrow expressed in this song? These people had lost their homes, were taken from the land that had been promised to them by God and relocated in a strange land.

Many of them had been separated from family members and placed into a culture completely contrary to the culture of Zion. Their freedom had been taken from them, their dreams lay in the ashes of the burned-out remnants of the city of Jerusalem.

The next generations would never experience the majesty of worshiping Jehovah in the temple built by Solomon, a temple that now lay in ruins, stripped of all its treasure, all its glory. As they sat by the rivers of Babylon, everything familiar and comforting was becoming a distant memory and they felt the weight of all they had lost. The stress and sorrow was unbearable. So they wept.

There are some losses worth weeping over.

June 20, 2009, is a date that will live forever in my memory. It has left a mark on my soul like no other. There may be times that my birthday will come and go without me giving it much thought, but that day, the day before Father's Day, 2009, will never go unnoticed. It was the day this father suffered his greatest loss.

The first phone call came as I was enjoying a day with my oldest son, Jeremy, at Infineon Raceway, located about 45 minutes from my home. Jeremy had secured passes to the VIP tent sponsored by Red Bull and we were anticipating a day of watching the greatest racing names in NASCAR. We were watching them go through their practice rounds in preparation for the race that was to take place the next day. The sound from my phone interrupted that wondrous moment.

"Dave, this is Deb," she said with some concern in her voice. "I wanted to let you know that Amy fainted as Karen and I were getting her into the car this morning." Amy, my

31-year-old daughter, was in the third day of recovering from surgery, and Karen, one of Amy's close friends, had come to the house to help Deborah take Amy to a follow-up appointment with the surgeon.

The surgery had gone well and Amy was recovering ahead of schedule. However, she needed help in moving from the chair in our living room where she had been sleeping to the car in the garage.

It was difficult to hear Deborah's voice over the roar of the cars on the racetrack. As I pushed the phone harder to my ear I was barely able to hear Deb say that she had called an ambulance and Amy was at the hospital being checked out by the doctors.

She didn't think I needed to come home and she assured me that she would call when she knew more. The call left me a little uneasy, but after telling Jeremy about the call we went back to watching the cars go through their paces. Even though I enjoyed watching the cars fly around the racetrack, I was eager to get the call that would confirm what I was sure would be good news.

It wasn't very long before the second call came. This time it wasn't Deborah. It was Karen. Her voice was shaky and it was obvious that she was fighting back deep emotion.

"Dave, this is Karen. You need to come home immediately. Amy isn't doing well and the doctors don't think she's going to make it." I was stunned and couldn't believe the words I was hearing. This could not be possible. Not my Amy, not my daughter!

"What happened?" I asked, as if knowing more about the situation would help me affect the outcome. Karen didn't have an explanation. The doctors were not even sure what had happened. All they knew was that she was not breathing and they couldn't resuscitate her. I ended the call telling Karen I was on my way and asking her to let Deb know I was coming.

After giving Jeremy the news and asking him to pray and call others to pray, I ran to the dirt parking field praying with desperation greater than I knew was possible. The parking lot, mostly empty when I had arrived earlier that morning, now was packed. I must have wandered up and down the rows of cars for ten minutes crying out to God to help me find my small convertible before I stumbled on it, hidden between two large SUVs.

The drive to the hospital was surreal. I was both numb and manic at the same time. Though my mind could not believe that my daughter might be dead, my emotions and imagination were actively fighting to bring me to its probability. I envisioned Amy's fear in the moments leading to her death. I anguished over what I imagined Deborah was going through. I was overwhelmed by the thought of Amy's two young children. How would they survive the news of their mother's death? I was afraid that this news would only bring them years of sorrow and grief.

At the same time, there were the questions that fought for space in my already crowded thoughts. What would this mean for our family? What will happen to Amy's children? What will it feel like to stand at my own daughter's gravesite? How will it be possible to comfort Deborah?

In the midst of all this internal turmoil, my physical voice was not silent the entire trip to Vacaville. I prayed loudly in every way I knew how. I pleaded, begged, demanded, thanked, praised, but mostly declared life over my daughter. By the time I reached the hospital, my voice was raspy from the intensity and volume of my supplication. I cannot tell you that I *felt* the comfort of the Holy Spirit, but I can tell you that I am confident He was present and active, for I would not have survived the chaos of that drive home without Him.

Deb's journey to the hospital that day started as I mentioned with Amy passing out on the garage floor while being helped to the car. Amy had awakened that morning feeling better than expected and she, Deb, and Karen anticipated an uneventful morning of getting her to the surgeon's for a routine examination.

Deb and Karen helped Amy up on her feet and walked out to the car, one of them behind her and one in front. When they got to the car, Amy collapsed without warning and fell to the ground. The two women had to act quickly to keep her from hitting her head on the concrete. Though they hoped it was only a fainting spell from being inactive for a few days, they immediately called 911 and the ambulance arrived within a few minutes.

When the paramedics arrived they worked on her for a short time but got very little response, so they quickly transported her to the hospital only a mile or so from our home.

When Deborah arrived at the emergency room she took care of the necessary paperwork that the hospital required. Then, she called me to let me know what was going on, and that she was still waiting to hear from either the doctors or nurses.

It was a long time before a nurse came into the waiting room and asked Deb to follow her into another room where, she said, "We need to talk." Karen accompanied Deb into the room, the reality that something was terribly wrong dawning on both.

The nurse quietly told Deb the doctors were continuing to work on Amy. She was being purposefully obscure in her description of what was going on in the other room when Deb interrupted her and said, "I want you to tell me my daughter is going to be OK." The nurse hesitated, and then responded with regret and compassion, "I can't tell you that."

The nurse then asked, "Do you know what a Code Blue is?" Deb's heart sank as she responded, "I know exactly what it is." Deborah and Karen sat stunned as the nurse excused herself from the room.

It wasn't long before the nurse came back to Deborah and Karen and told Deborah that Amy was not responding and asked if she would like to see her daughter. Deborah didn't hesitate and was led into the emergency room where the teams of doctors were just giving up on resuscitating Amy. It was evident to Deborah that they had done everything humanly possible to save Amy's life and were devastated by the result. Deb took her daughter into her arms and wept.

When I arrived at the hospital emergency entrance a nurse took me to a darkened room where I found Deborah sitting in a chair, resting her head on the gurney Amy was laying on. She had one arm draped around her daughter's waist, and I could hear her quietly crying. I walked over to

Deborah and put one arm around her and my other arm on my daughter. I whispered the question no father should ever have to ask, "Is Amy gone?" I heard the words that no father should hear as Deborah softly spoke the words no mother should ever have to say, "Yes, she's gone."

Hanging Up Your Harps

Yes, there are some losses worth weeping over. Everyone experiences their own Babylon—the place where opposing circumstances, difficulties, tragedies, and devastating losses conspire to rob us of our freedom, our dreams, and our authentic life message. However, our life message need never be hostage to our losses.

The name Babylon comes from the word *Babel,* which means to confound, bewilder, and confuse. Babylon is designed by the enemy to hold our hearts captive and steal our true identity. That is exactly what happened to those written about in the verses of Psalm 137. Listen to the confession of their song.

> *By the rivers of Babylon, there we sat down, yea, we wept when we remembered Zion. We hung our harps upon the willows in the midst of it, for there those who carried us away captive asked of us a song. And those who plundered us requested mirth, saying, 'sing us one of the songs of Zion.' How shall we sing the Lord's song in a foreign land?* (Psalm 137:1-4)

Notice the following two phrases: "We hung our harps upon the willows…" and "How shall we sing the Lord's song in a foreign land?"

It is my contention that the last thing they should have done is to hang their harps on the willows and refuse to sing the Lord's song. In so doing they gave up their dreams, lost their identity, and perverted their life message. Let me explain.

The nation of Israel was chosen by God to represent or re-present Him to other nations and people. The children of Israel were carriers of divine revelation, the people of God's favor. They had a history that was replete with stories containing signs, wonders, and miracles. They experienced and understood the power of redemption. And even though their rebellion led to their captivity they still possessed the song of the Lord. That song should have been sung in a way that would cause jealousy among the nations.

It was God's ultimate purpose to reveal Himself through the children of Israel. It was His hope that this revelation would be for the purpose of blessing those nations. This divine purpose is powerfully expressed in Jehovah's declaration to Isaac:

> *And I will make your descendants multiply as the stars of heaven; I will give to your descendants all these lands; and in your seed all the nations of the earth shall be blessed* (Genesis 26:4).

What better place to tune the harp and sing the song of the Lord than in a foreign land. If there was any nation that needed a revelation of God it was Babylon, and these Jews carried that revelation. They had the opportunity of a lifetime to be a transformational agent for a nation in need of God. Instead, they were overcome by their circumstances, hanging their harps on the willow, and giving up their identity and ultimately devaluing their legacy.

THE POWER OF ONE

Thankfully, there were a few among the children of Israel that did not cease to sing the song of the Lord. One of those who refused to hang up his harp was Daniel. Daniel was a young boy of 14 to 16 years of age when he was taken from Jerusalem to Babylon. He came from a royal family raised in comfort and favor. When he arrived in Babylon, he was placed in an environment designed to strip his identity, his culture, and his original life message.

The Babylonians started their indoctrination of Daniel by changing his name from Daniel, meaning "God is my judge" to Belteshazzar, meaning "the treasure of Bel." They insisted that he eat the food that was defiled and, at the same time, trained him in the wisdom of the Chaldeans. If there was ever anyone put under pressure to give up his identity it was Daniel. Yet, he refused to stop singing the song of the Lord.

His commitment would bring him in conflict with the king. Out of jealousy and in an effort to trap Daniel, some of the king's advisors convinced the king to sign a decree that for the next 40 days people could pray only to the king. If they prayed to any other person or deity they would be punished and thrown into a den of lions. They knew that Daniel would only pray to his God. Though the king loved Daniel, he had no choice but to have him thrown to the lions when he was informed of Daniel's disobedience. Early the next morning, he ran to the lion's den to see if Daniel survived the night. To his delight, his God had preserved Daniel. The impact of Daniel's life message is reflected in the new decree uttered by the king.

Peace and prosperity to you! I decree that everyone throughout my kingdom should tremble with fear before the God of Daniel. For he is the living God and he will endure forever. His kingdom will never be destroyed, and his rule will never end. He rescues and saves his people; he performs miraculous signs and wonders in the heavens and on earth. He has rescued Daniel from the power of the lions (Daniel 6:25-27 NLT).

Daniel used his God-given gifts and favor to bless the nation that held him captive. Those gifts would, in turn, captivate the nation. Even when his life was threatened because of the jealousy of the governmental leaders around him, Daniel chose to never give up and give in to those pressures. He threw open his window three times a day, worshiped God, and risked death rather than hang his harp on the willow.

These actions fulfilled his destiny as a child of God. His faithfulness to God would cause him to influence the Babylonians, even those at the highest levels of government. Ultimately, a legacy was born—a legacy of a man whose life message would continue to reverberate down the halls of history to this very day.

You Have a Choice

Every conflicting circumstance that enters your life, every Babylon, no matter how daunting or bewildering, contains a choice. You can either choose to hang your harp on the willow—or throw open the window; stop singing your song—or turn up the volume of your worship and praise. We can let our life message be held in the captivity of our circumstances or we can choose to walk in our destiny.

It is important to understand that I am not talking about making the best of a bad situation. What I am speaking of is an opportunity to transform our Babylon—a place of confusion and devastation—into a Bethel, the house of God.

As people of God, we are called to be agents of transformation in whatever set of circumstances we are in. We have the one who created the universe living in us and wanting to flow through us. We can choose to let our losses dominate our message, or we release the power in us as an expression of the "exceedingly abundantly above all we ask or think."

When Deb and I walked away from the hospital that day, leaving our daughter's body to be taken to the county morgue, we experienced a level of grief I didn't know was possible. Our hearts physically ached and we felt a pain so deep that we couldn't breathe. We wept more than I thought possible.

In that moment of a grief impinging on our desperate souls, we were confronted with a choice that every Babylon presents. Before we reached the car in the hospital parking lot a resolve was already rising in our hearts. We verbalized some of it to each other even as we pulled out of the parking lot. At that moment the words were not quite there but over the ensuing weeks we have found some language for that resolve.

I share it here, not as a testimony of our strength, but as a testimony of the Father's goodness. We came to understand that we must hold ourselves accountable for the choices we are making in this time of our greatest loss. Here is the content of that resolution that was massaged into our spirits.

We resolve that we will not sacrifice our destiny or our life message on the altar of our grief.

We resolve that we will not exchange the joy of the Father for a life of anger, bitterness, or sadness.

We resolve that the part of our legacy that comes out of this experience will be that our later years were greater than our former and that at the place of our deepest loss we choose to become better people.

We resolve that we will turn every place of sorrow into a spring of refreshing; that in every disappointment we will raise the volume of our worship; and in the face of every opposition we will tune our harps and sing the song of the Lord.

We resolve that our life message will never be held hostage to our loss.

We resolve that our Babylon will become our Bethel.

CHAPTER NINE

Turning Babylon into Bethel

*"The strongest principle of growth
lies in human choice."*—George Elliot

*A*s I stated in the previous chapter, everyone will experience a Babylon. Once we are there we wonder how did we get there? Sometimes, it is a result of our own poor decisions. Those decisions lead us to a place where we are confronted by circumstances trying to strip our life message from us. But it is not always bad choices or wrong actions that get us into Babylon. There are times when it is simply the result of being human and living in an imperfect world.

The cause is not as important as the choices and reactions we make when we are living in Babylon. We may be going through a Babylon experience, but our heart, our dreams, and our life message need not be held in captivity.

In Psalm 137 the Jewish people chose to react negatively to their circumstances in Babylon, the place of their captivity.

Those reactions and choices flowed out of their hearts—the seat of all the issues of life.

- They chose to believe in the power of their present circumstances rather than the promises and character of God.

- They chose to declare their condition rather than their identity.

- They chose to remember what was lost rather than their God-given destiny.

- They chose to delight in their lost glory rather than the God of Glory.

These choices made their physical captivity into a spiritual captivity—a captivity of the heart. Confusion and disappointment became their dwelling place. It didn't have to happen. There were other ways to confront their circumstances.

What we choose to believe determines the state of our mind and the growth in our spirits. What we declare, remember, and delight in can set our heart free to explore, discover, dream, and grow even in the most difficult of circumstance.

Our testimony expressed in Babylon will have a great influence on this generation. What should be the nature of that testimony? It is the voice of the redeemed, the language of the Spirit, and the songs of those who know their God. We owe it to our families and the world we live in to keep our hearts out of Babylon. Just because we are living in Babylon, we don't have to let Babylon live in us.

In my life I have discovered some important keys that have helped me to transform my Babylon into Bethel.

BELIEVE

Belief opens doors and positions us in a place where we are moving in the right direction, avoiding dark alleys and dead ends. This spiritual faith puts us on a path that will lead us to correct conclusions based on that belief. As Christians we are called "believers." To be a believer means that we believe in something. Therefore, the appropriate question to ask ourselves is, "What do we believe?"

In Israel's case they believed their circumstances had greater power than their promises. This perspective allowed their circumstance to have great control over their lives. In the grip of those circumstances they abandoned their destiny and the power of their influence. They hung their harps on the willow.

The decision to discard their harps and ditch the song of the Lord in this strange land had a cataclysmic impact upon their spirits. By choosing to believe the wrong thing they were seduced into negativity and despondency.

When we choose to believe that the power of God's promises can alter our circumstances we will move into a better place—a place where our circumstance become a predictor of our promises coming true. How can we know this?

Here is another discovery I have made. It seems that with every promise we receive it is usually accompanied with an opposing circumstance, seeking to discredit the promise. In the face of that circumstance we chose to believe that all things really do work for the good of those that love God and are called to His purposes. As we focus our faith on the promise, rather than the circumstances, our faith rises and our perspectives are adjusted as our life follows the path established by our belief.

Believing what Heaven says about us, which is our true identity, gives us boldness to step into that realm of freedom where anything is possible. Believing that we are who He says we are releases our heavenly potential. It is critical that we choose to believe what Heaven says rather than what our circumstances appear to dictate.

Belief unlocks the realm of the impossible, causes our heart to be enlarged and our life message to be transformed and transforming. William Blake said that in the universe, there are things that are known, and things that are unknown, and in between, there are doors. Our belief will help us to find those doors.

In the play *The Man of La Mancha*, Don Quixote, an old man with little hold on reality, sets out to right the wrongs he perceives that exist around him. He sees a windmill and believes it is a four-armed giant, so he attacks it. He comes across a run-down roadside inn and imagines it to be a glorious castle. His servant, Sancho, is constantly trying to help Don understand that what he sees or believes is not real. Unfortunately, he did not have much success.

As the story continues, they enter the roadside inn that Quixote believes to be a castle and inside they find a worn-out barmaid and prostitute named Aldonza. Quixote believes her to be a beautiful lady and names her Dulcinea and treats her in the manner due a lady. She believes him to be crazy.

During the course of Quixote's stay at the inn, Aldonza is terribly mistreated by some of the patrons and Don swears to avenge his Lady Dulcinea. Aldonza begs Quixote to leave her alone, continuing to believe herself a barmaid and he an idiot.

The Knights of the Mirror, men from Quixote's hometown, show up at the inn and force him to see himself the way the world sees him—a fool and a madman. During the confrontation, Don Quixote collapses. He is taken back to his home where he lapses into a coma. When he awakens he is in his right mind and desires to make out his will.

A woman enters the room where others have gathered to assist Quixote. It is obvious from her beautiful clothes, her dignity, and charm that she is in every way a lady. Don Quixote does not recognize her until she introduces herself as Dulcinea.

Aldonza, the prostitute and barmaid, had become what Don Quixote believed her to be. How can this be? This story powerfully illustrates my point. By choosing to believe in the identity Quixote had given her, she was transformed into that picture. Belief unlocked the impossible dream, opened a door for her, and transformed her life message from Aldonza into Dulcinea.

This is a fictional story that has its roots in spiritual reality. Let me explain it this way. There was a time in my life that I never could believe that I would ever write a book. But when I chose to believe the prophetic words over my life that I was going to write, I became a writer. I chose to ignore my feelings and accept the word over me. Belief transforms. It realigns your world and brings it into alignment with your God-given identity.

When we choose to believe that God is for us and not against us, that belief opens our hearts and influences our minds to accept the limitless possibilities before us as it also releases us from the fear of failure. Believing that God is faithful frees hearts from the dread of disappointment and grants the courage to risk what we believe. Believing that He is good liberates us from the fear of being used or manipulated, making us vulnerable to His love, leading to greater confidence and hope.

David makes this confession in Psalm 27:13:

What would have become of me had I not believed that I would see the Lord's goodness in the land of the living (Psalm 27:13 AMP).

Deb and I can legitimately confess this verse as our own. Believing that God is good has been the anchor of our lives during the storm that confronted us with the death of our daughter. We cannot even begin to imagine what would have become of us if this basic and critical belief had not been the centerpiece of our heart. Jesus put it this way, *"Out of the abundance of the heart the mouth speaks"* (Matt. 12:34). This is never truer than in the times of great crises. In times of trouble, what is in our hearts becomes exposed through our words. The reality of our beliefs is challenged by the disturbances of life.

When Deborah entered the room where the doctors had so valiantly worked to save Amy's life, the reality that her daughter was dead crashed over her like a tsunami. As she seated herself next to the gurney and laid her head and arms over the lifeless body of her best friend and only daughter, she could not have predicted what words would come out of her mouth. There was no way to rehearse this situation. What was already in her heart would pour forth from her lips as she whispered through her tears, "God, you're good."

When you are confronted by tragedy what will you choose to believe?

DECLARATION

The word *virtual* is defined as "existing or resulting in essence or effect, though not in actual fact." In the moment that Deborah whispered, "God, you're good," the goodness of God was not a virtual reality. It was an actual fact. It was not a religious slogan, but a declaration made from the depths of her being. That declaration of God's goodness was already the foundation on which Deborah stood, without wavering, while the world around her crumbled.

Words are very important and the declarations we make are powerful expressions of the heart and of our faith. In the Kingdom of God they are indispensable tools of activation. Abraham Heschel said that words create worlds. The words we declare have power to create worlds where God can act.

In Genesis 1 we see the Spirit of the Lord hovering over the earth that is formless, empty and without light. "And God *said* (declared), *"Let there be light," and there was light"* (Gen. 1:1 NIV). It is interesting that the world was dark and empty until the word was spoken. The word of God activated the will of God.

Declarations are like seeds that we deposit into the soil of life and those deposits of declarations will produce fruit after its own kind. Declarations have the power to enslave or liberate, signal death or give birth. A negative declaration will produce negative fruit and a positive declaration will produce positive fruit. A seed will always produce according to its DNA. We must come to the place where we comprehend the power of our declarations.

The Jews that were in captivity in Babylon made their declarations visible with their actions and audible with their voice. Hanging their harps on the willow and stating, "How can we sing the song of the Lord in a foreign land" are declarations that contain the seeds of despair, producing the fruit of surrender and defeat. Their declarations ultimately led to their loss of influence and identity.

When we make a declaration we come into agreement with one of two kingdoms, the Kingdom of God or the kingdom of darkness. Each *amen* we declare has a corresponding result. Declarations that are made with faith and in agreement with the word of God will receive a resounding and corresponding "Amen" from Heaven, releasing the resource of Heaven and the influence of His kingdom. We invite Heaven into our circumstances by the words we speak and the declarations we make.

Those that come into agreement with doubt and unbelief receive the "amen" from the kingdom of darkness and the resulting release of its caustic atmosphere and influence. No wonder Scripture makes the powerful statement, *"Death and life are in the power of the tongue"* (Prov. 18:21 KJV).

On the three-month anniversary of Amy's death, Graham Cooke spoke in the Sunday morning service. I don't believe he was aware it was an anniversary date, but he made reference to our loss and some other difficulties that our community was experiencing. Listen to his words: "We (The Mission community) have taken some hard hits, *but we are still here, and we are not going away.*" This was a declaration in agreement with the Kingdom of God. When Graham spoke these words everyone immediately felt a shift in the atmosphere and a marshalling of the forces of Heaven on our behalf. Personally, I sensed the applause of the angels in the room and I felt my inner man rise up and my resolve stiffen. I am not going away.

Babylon has a loud voice, and the volume of opposing circumstances can be deafening. However, declarations rooted in the character and nature of God silences the scream of opposition and replaces it with the quite, confident voice of the Holy Spirit. Listen to the confidence that comes from the heart of David following his opening declaration of Psalm 27:1-3:

> *The Lord is my light and my salvation; whom shall I fear? Though an host may encamp against me, my heart shall not fear; though war may rise against me, in this I will be confident* (Psalm 27:1-3 KJV).

Remember

Memories play an important part in our lives. Someone once said that memories are the treasures that we keep locked deep within the storehouse of our souls, to keep our hearts warm when we are lonely.

Memories feed our faith. Several times in Scripture God reminds His people to remember Him, His works, and His words. There were times when He told the nation of Israel to build altars of remembrance so they would be reminded for generations of God's deliverance of His people.

Not all memories warm the soul. There are some memories that freeze us in the past and are limiting and debilitating. These kinds of memories, when dwelt upon, can hold us back and keep us from our future. Sometimes it is not just remembering the event, but rather the way we remember the event that keeps us in Babylon. This was the case with Israel.

Remembering Zion seems like a good thing to remember. Zion represented the place of God's promise and their destiny. Remembering it this way would inspire hope and give them courage. But this is not how they remembered Zion. They remember only what they had lost, not what they were promised. By choosing to remember what they had lost they got lost in a maze of discouragement and hopelessness.

Let me say again, there are some losses worthy of tears, many tears. But how we choose to remember those losses can lead us into bondage or celebration.

A few weeks after we buried our daughter, Deb and I took some time in Hawaii to rest and heal. Hawaii has always been a place of renewal for us and we were thankful we could get away. The time was helpful, but also contained some very difficult experiences. In a time of grief, pleasant memories are often the most painful, and we had many memories of times in Hawaii with Amy. Each time we ran into those memories they reminded us of what would never be again.

They also challenged us to remember in a way that would release joy, not just tears.

One of the most difficult memories for me was an occurrence that connected to one of the sweetest memories I have of Amy.

When Amy was graduating from junior high, several of us fathers from the Mission took our daughters to dinner on Pier 39 in San Francisco to celebrate their accomplishment. It was a delightful evening, and my favorite memory of that night was a purchase I made for Amy at a pearl kiosk as we walked to the restaurant. In order to purchase a pearl you select an oyster to be opened by the salesperson. The pearl inside your selected oyster is the one you can have mounted on jewelry or just kept as is. I always took great delight when buying gifts for Amy, mostly because she so enjoyed receiving them. This time was especially pleasurable as I watched her enthusiastically choose her oyster and celebrate the pearl inside. That pearl remains in Amy's jewelry collection to this day.

These pearl kiosks can be found in many tourist locations, including Hawaii. Following dinner one evening, after we enjoyed a delicious meal and a magnificent sunset, Deb and I were walking through the shopping area of Whalers Village on our way to the car. We arrived near one of those kiosks at the very moment a couple of young girls with their parents were so excited about the pearl they had found in their oysters. I was instantly taken back to that moment in San Francisco and the memory rushed in like a flood. I was devastated. I'm not sure how I kept walking toward the parking lot, but somehow I made my way to the car, got in, and backed it out of its parking spot. But as the car began to move forward I lost all composure and began to weep violently.

I don't know how we did it but we made it back to our condo emotionally drained and wondering how one of the most precious memories I have of Amy could become the most painful.

I was angry when I realized that a valuable thing had been stolen from me. That night, Deb and I decided we were not going to allow that to happen again. It has not been easy, but we choose not to remember what we lost, but to celebrate the joy of what we had experienced.

The first test of our resolve, for me, came a few days later when we again walked past that kiosk on our way to dinner in Whalers Village. As we approached it, I intentionally looked at it and gave thanks for that wonderful moment in San Francisco when I indulged my daughter. This time, instead of deep pain, there was peace. Oh, there was still a sense of loss, but it was unable to steal from me the joy of that memory, or the enjoyment of the Maui sunset. My Babylon had become a Bethel, a place of meeting with my God.

A memory can be a call to worship or a downbeat for the melancholy music of a funeral dirge. It is either the motivation to play and sing the song of the Lord or it is the last straw that causes us to hang up our instruments and mourn our losses. The same memory can be a call to battle or a flag of surrender. The choice is ours.

We can choose to remember in a way that restricts our growth and shuts down our dreams or, we can remember in a way that stimulates our advancement into greater possibilities and increases the impact of our life message. Releasing our memory in the right way unlocks the impossible, inspires hope, and ignites our faith.

As for Deb and me, we are choosing to remember those things that open our heart to wonder and amazement, and remember everything in a way that sets our hearts free to dream.

DELIGHT

David discovered one of the secrets to keeping one's heart from being held captive by circumstances. In Psalm 37:4 is the lyrics of a song that he wrote about that secret: *"Delight yourself also in the Lord and he will give you the desires of your heart."* David is making it plain that we have permission to personally take pleasure in the Lord, and in so doing He partners with us to fulfill the desires and longings of our heart.

To delight in something is to take pleasure in something, to celebrate the joy found in something we give value to. When we read farther down in the Psalm 137:5, we discover what the people chose to delight in.

> *If I forget you, O Jerusalem, let my right hand forget its skill. If I do not remember you, let my tongue cling to the roof of my mouth – if I do not exalt Jerusalem above my chief joy* (Psalm 137:5).

This sounds noble, even spiritual, until we recognize that they were focusing on the wrong thing. They had chosen to take joy in their lost glory over the God of glory. What should be the "chief joy" of the people of Israel, the city of David or the God of David? By choosing the lesser glory their hearts remained in bondage to the circumstances around them. Had they chosen to take their delight in their relationship with the God of Abraham, Isaac, and Jacob, their hearts would be free, even though their physicality was still held captive.

Tim May, one of our team members at The Mission, has a vibrant ministry in several prisons in California, including the prison in Vacaville. The men he and his team minister to are held in captivity, herded like cattle and every detail of life is under observation. They are told what to eat and when to eat; where to sleep and when to sleep. These men are literally in prison. Tim often shares with me that, in spite of being in prison, some of these men have chosen to delight themselves in Jesus Christ. Their delight in the Lord has given them a freedom of heart that no guard or prison cell can take away.

Taking delight in the Lord is not a religious thought or a passive activity. It is an intentional decision to live in the realm of His favor and to permit ourselves the pleasure of all He is and does. Delighting in the Lord is like exercising our physical muscles.

We exercise our "delight" through confession, thanksgiving, and declaring the goodness of the Lord. In this way we direct our delight to the place that keeps our heart pure and free as we partner with the Father. The following is a declaration of my delight that I find helpful.

> Father I delight myself in you today. I delight myself in your love, your mercy, your compassion, and your faithfulness. I delight myself in the day you have designed for me, in the opportunities you have made available, and in the promises you are fulfilling in this day. I delight myself in your goodness, I delight myself in you.

I am going to end this chapter with a story I think you will find delightful.

As I mentioned earlier in this chapter, Deborah and I took some time away in Hawaii following our daughter's passing. It was a vacation we already had on the calendar and came at an opportune time. However, because of what we were going through we decided to go five days earlier than scheduled. In scheduling a condo for those extra days we chose the Kapalua Villas, a resort north of where we usually stay.

I booked the least expensive villa, one tucked up in the golf course with a "fairway view." When we arrived to check in to the villa, the receptionist informed us that they had upgraded us to a "Gold" villa—a unit that had been completely renovated and updated. We were thankful for the upgrade and upon entering the villa we became very excited about the beautiful and inviting accommodations. Even the view of the golf course in the foreground and the Pacific Ocean on the horizon was more than we expected. Little did we know what the Father had in mind for us. There is more to the story.

It was around seven in the evening by the time we unpacked our clothes and settled into the comfortable living room furniture, reading our favorite novels. The phone rang breaking the sweetness of the moment. It was the front desk. The receptionist that had welcomed us on our arrival came quickly to the point of her call. "Mr. Crone, we would like to upgrade you to an Ocean View Villa." Though this sounded good, we had already unpacked, were tired from the trip and to be honest, quite happy with the condo we were settled into. My response was simply, "I'll talk to my wife and call you back." After talking with Deb we agreed that we were content where we were and decided to stay put.

When I called the receptionist and gave her our answer, her response surprised me. "Will you at least let us show you a couple of units and then you can decide?" It did seem intriguing so we told her we would look. A few minutes later a van showed up at our door and a young man took us down near the ocean and showed us a couple of units with ocean views. One of the units did have a very beautiful view, but it was obvious that the unit was not a "Gold" unit. The furnishings in the living room were very sparse and uncomfortable, and at this point in our journey, we needed somewhere we could be comfortable and just relax.

We returned to our original unit, called the front desk, thanked the receptionist for the offer but informed her we would stay where we were. Again, her response surprised me and this time raised my suspicion that something was up. "Will you let us show you some more units that have the furnishings you're looking for?" My curiosity and suspicion got the best of me and I said, "Obviously you have a problem and need us to help you resolve it. Is that right?"

"Yes," she said. She went on to explain that the owner of the unit we were occupying had unexpectantly arrived and was demanding the use of his own condo. No matter how much the receptionist explained the situation, the owner continued to insist on getting *his* condo.

As we finally understood the situation, Deb and I let her know that if she could find a comparable unit, no matter where it was, we would be willing to make a move. The receptionist was greatly relieved and promised to find such a unit and provide help for us to move our luggage. While she looked for another unit we repacked our suitcases. It was now about 8:00 P.M. Hawaii time, 11:00 P.M. our west coast time. We were exhausted.

It wasn't long until the van pulled up and a pleasant woman greeted us, helped us carry our luggage to the van, and transported us down to the ocean-front condos that lined the bay. When we stepped into the unit we were immediately overwhelmed. To say that this was a "Gold" unit would be an understatement. The unit set right above the beach and the entire front of the condo, kitchen, dining room, and living room, had a panoramic view of the Pacific Ocean, the majestic Fleming Beach and the beautiful Honolua Bay.

The beach was a one-minute walk from the front door. The furnishings of this ocean front condo were stunning in their quality and comfort. Everything about it was first-class and luxurious. It was exceedingly, abundantly, above and beyond what we could ask or think.

Those five days were an embrace from the Father. He manifested His goodness, and indulged himself on two of His children. The whole experience was as if the Father was insisting—"You will be upgraded." That is just like the Father we know, and we take our exquisite delight in Him. You never know what might happen when you begin to delight yourself in the Lord. Your prison could be transformed into an extravagant Hawaiian condo!

SECTION TWO

The Impact

The discovery and development of one's life message leaves a mark, not only on the individual, but on his family and community. The remaining chapters of this book speak to mind-sets and approaches to life and faith that have been impacted as we have pursued our life message as a community of believers, dreamers, and friends.

CHAPTER TEN

Decisions That Define Us

"Decisions determine destiny."
—Frederick Speakman

I sat at my desk on a Saturday afternoon in May of 2004 contemplating what I would share with students graduating the next day from our Potter's House School of the Supernatural. As I was reflecting on our journey as a community, a number of decisions made during that journey began to erupt out of my spirit and find their way through my fingers and onto the computer screen in front of me. As I read them aloud to myself, and then to the students and church the next day, it was evident that these were values that had come to define our church community and declarations of our life message.

Since then, the document, "Decisions That Define Us," has circulated globally via the Internet, resonating within the hearts of leaders and church communities around the world.

Before you read these decisions it is important for you to understand the context. These are not and never were a reaction to anything but the state of our own hearts and the reality in our church. They are absolutely in no way a criticism of any church or denominational movement. We are in this battle for high ground together: one Church, one Bride, and one Body.

We would probably have said these decisions were true from the beginning of our ministry. Now, however, they are points of contention, foundational values without which we are not willing to live.

In Second Samuel 6, as David leads the return of the Ark of the Covenant, there is both celebration and sacrifice; and so it is with these commitments. As we are heeding the ever-increasing call to clear a path for the manifest presence and glory of God, these decisions have each taken a piece out of our hearts and lives and given us something priceless in return.

Mile Markers

So, then, here are the Decisions that Define Us:

We have decided that teaching the gospel without demonstrating the gospel is not enough. Good preaching, good doctrine, and being good people are not enough.

We have decided that having a good church club is not enough, good fellowship is not enough, and just being a member of that club is not enough.

We have decided that having good Bible studies is good, but not good enough, that just making it to Heaven is not our goal, and that knowing about God without truly knowing and experiencing God is meaningless.

We have decided that having good programs is not enough, that change without transformation is intolerable, and that staying where we are is not an option.

We have decided that gifting without character is futile.

We have decided that singing songs without worshiping is empty, and having meetings without God showing up is pointless.

We have decided that having faith without works is not enough and having works without love is not acceptable—that our function comes out of our relationship first with the Father and second with each other.

We have decided that reading about the Book of Acts without living the Book of Acts is unthinkable.

We have decided that confident faith is good and bold faith is better.

We have decided that hearing about the Holy Spirit without experiencing Him is silly, that believing in His presence without seeing it manifested in signs and wonders is hypocrisy, that believing in healing without seeing people healed is absurd, and that believing in deliverance without people being delivered is absolutely ridiculous.

We have decided to be Holy Spirit filled, Holy Spirit led, and Holy Spirit empowered—anything less doesn't work for us.

We have decided to be the ones telling the stories of God's power—not the ones hearing about them.

We have decided that living saved but not supernatural is living below our privilege and short of what Christ died for.

We have decided that we are a battle ship not a cruise ship, an army not an audience, Special Forces not spectators, missionaries not club members.

We have decided to value both pioneers and settlers: pioneers to expand our territory and settlers to build on those territories. But we are not squatters, people who take up space others have fought for without improving it.

We have decided to be infectious instead of innocuous, contagious instead of quarantined, deadly instead of benign.

We have decided to be radical lovers and outrageous givers.

We have decided that we are a mission station and not a museum.

We have decided that it is better to fail while reaching for the impossible that God has planned for us than to succeed settling for less.

We have decided that nothing short of His Kingdom coming and His will being done in our world as it is in Heaven will satisfy.

We have decided that we will not be satisfied until our world cries out, *"These who have turned the world upside down have come here too"* (Acts 17:6).

These are some of the decisions that define who we are as a community and how we choose to live our lives.

These decisions are not destinations, but rather journeys—journeys along an ancient path. We have not found some new way. We discovered an avenue as old as Abraham, Isaac, and Jacob, traveled by Moses, Joshua, and Caleb. On this same risky road, Paul, John, and Peter paved the way for the first century church, a church that revolutionized the culture of the first century and beyond.

It is an adventure that will impact our world today. It is a path of Bold Faith—believing that what God says is really true and acting on it; Outrageous Generosity—giving our life away in order to demonstrate His Kingdom; Radical Love—loving God with everything in us and our neighbor as ourselves.

It is a life of liberty, freedom, and healing, where you will find significance, purpose, and destiny. This is a path less traveled. However, it is not a journey available only to a select few; anyone may come on this highway cut by the hand of God for people of every nation, tribe, and tongue, for those in any occupation or vocation.

No matter where you are in your life journey, there is room on this path for you.

Decisions that define us are not arrogant proclamations of our accomplishments; they are fresh commitments to pursue Jesus' teachings and actions. We know that there are many more decisions to be made that will continue to define our life message. There is still so much more ground to contend for. We continue to comprehend the high cost and great value of each declaration of purpose, while remaining humbly aware that Jesus paid the price that made possible the events of the Book of Acts—then and now.

Chapter Eleven

Greater Than Excellence

"God save us from an explainable life."
—Cleddie Keith

*E*xcellence is a worthy pursuit. The opposite has been welcomed in the life of the church for too long. If you have attended church for as long as I have, you have at some point painfully endured a "special" solo on a Sunday morning that had not been well-rehearsed, or a drama that was poorly written and badly acted. I remember when I was a young man and our church took a food offering for a couple who had just joined the church staff. What came in for this young couple from the cupboards of the church members could be generously described as their leftovers, less generously as their unwanted garbage. Missionaries have often had to endure the castoffs of others and pastors have had to struggle to live with less than enough to care for their families. It is as if mediocrity has been celebrated as humility. Thankfully this is changing in much of the church world.

One of the things I love about our team at The Mission is their pursuit of excellence. Bob Book, our worship and arts leader at The Mission, models this team value as well as any of us with his dogged insistence on taking what we have and pushing it to its highest potential. Everything from his approach to musical expression to the words he uses to describe his relationship with God is permeated with his passion to present to the Father the highest quality. What I love even more is that Bob and the others on the team offer their excellence in anticipation of that which is greater.

Excellence is defined by the *American Heritage Dictionary* as "The state, quality, or condition of excelling; superiority."[1] To pursue excellence is to develop what one has—talent, resources, time, gifts, abilities—and use them to the full potential of what is possible. Herein lies the point of this chapter. As important as excellence is, there is something greater—it is the impossible. Excellence takes us to the limit of what is possible, but as people of the Kingdom, we are called to pursue and live in the impossible.

What I am about to share in the rest of this chapter should not be understood as a suggestion to abandon excellence, but rather a plea not to stop there.

LIVING THE IMPOSSIBLE

When I first began to investigate the implications of NIS, my definition of that which was the opposite of "inferior things" was "things of excellence." This made perfect sense and certainly, as I have already stated, is not an insignificant objective. However, my perspective on this subject began to change when God messed with my thinking while

I was leading Chinese house-church leaders in an exercise on hearing God. In fact, every detail of that trip helped me see NIS in a greater way.

Dan McCollam and I had been covertly escorted to a small apartment in northern China to spend three days teaching and imparting to 20 or so pastors and church leaders. In order to protect the leaders, we could not be observed anywhere in or near the apartment, and the leaders could not be seen gathering in any significant numbers. Everything had been excellently planned by the church leaders, including our journey to the apartment, the way the leaders arrived each day, even the volume of our voices as we taught. For eight to ten hours a day, we had to teach in a whisper so that our American voices could not be heard outside the room. Even the Chinese had to be quiet so as to not draw attention to our gathering.

This was made especially difficult when, while teaching on the Holy Spirit, He decided to show up and the entire class began to feel and display the joy of the Lord in very loud and expressive ways. In our concern for their safety, Dan and I went around the room encouraging the leaders to get happy quietly and we were on the verge of questioning the wisdom of the Holy Spirit when things only got worse. The Holy Spirit didn't seem to care about our excellent planning! He just poured Himself out all the more on those precious believers. Inexplicably, we were not discovered. There were many things during our time in that apartment that could not be explained as the result of good planning. Let me share another example.

A Miraculous Exit

In planning our exit from the apartment, the Chinese believers, wanting to make it easier on us, planned to take us out of the meeting place in the morning, so that we would not have to move more than once before catching our train out of town.

Dan and I insisted that they be more concerned for their safety and less concerned about our comfort. It was decided that we would slip out of the apartment under the cover of darkness and get into a car that would take us to a hotel that caters to American tourists, making our presence less suspicious. The problem was that the public hallway leading from the apartment to the outside was well lit, as was the outside of the building where we were to get into the car. All it would take for these Christians to be in danger of arrest and possible imprisonment was for one person to open the door and see us in the hall, or an individual to walk by the outside of the building and catch a glimpse of us getting into the car.

When it came time to go and we were saying our tearful good-byes, the electricity for the entire city shut down. Total darkness enveloped the apartment building and the grounds around it. We were elated. God had made a way for our safe departure. Adding to our amazement was the fact that according to the leaders, this kind of power failure had never happened before. Though we saw this as the opportune time to go, the people didn't want us to leave and we spent several minutes praying over them some more and having them pray over us.

Before we could get away, the mother of the woman that owned the house stopped us from going and asked us to pray for her ankle. She had been in such pain that she could hardly walk. We tried to convince her that it would be better for us to leave and for others to pray for her, but she would not be dissuaded and we could not deny her. We prayed and she was completely healed. She went around excitedly showing everyone that she was pain-free. We quickly picked up our travel bags and headed for the door when the power suddenly came back on.

Disappointed that we had missed our window of opportunity, we once again said our good-byes, prayed, and tried to hold back our tears. Then, as if on cue, the power went off for a second time. This time we didn't hesitate, we bolted for the door, ran down the hall, out of the building, and into the waiting car, all under the cover of complete darkness. The power did not come back on until we were safely away from the apartment and in another part of the city.

Unexplainable, except by the supernatural that makes the impossible possible.

Now, let's go back to the revelation that came while training the leaders to hear God for themselves. In my book *Decisions that Define Us*, I share this story, but I believe it would be helpful to repeat it here.

RIGHT BETWEEN THE EYES

In one of our teaching times, we gave the leaders an exercise in hearing the Holy Spirit speak to them through a specific passage of Scripture. We had them meditate on Paul's prayer in Ephesians chapter three and record what they heard the Holy Spirit say to them.

I participated with them in the exercise by focusing on the last part of the prayer where Paul exclaims:

Now to Him who is able to do exceedingly abundantly above all that we ask or think, according to the power that works in us (Ephesians 3:20).

As I meditated, I began to get a picture of how big the dimension Paul described as beyond "all that we ask or think" really is. I sensed I was being invited by the Holy Spirit to explore this unknown and expansive territory. It struck me that this is the arena of the supernatural and it seemed to have no limitations. It is the place of the impossible—the place where dreams live.

Just as I was reveling in the possibilities of the impossible, I heard what I thought to be the Holy Spirit say, "But you know the limits of your personality." At first I agreed, but then I became angry and responded, "That's not fair! You made me with this personality and you can't limit my dreams just because of the way you chose to make me. You can't limit my potential by my abilities."

As my consternation continued to rise and my arguments became more emotional and less logical, I heard the Holy Spirit laughing as if to say, "Gotcha!" Jehovah Sneaky had goaded me into stepping out of my own limited mind-set and stepping into the place of dreaming dreams bigger than myself: above and beyond what I could ask or think.

A dear friend, Cleddie Keith, has often said, "God save us from an explainable life." I have adopted that prayer as my own. Excellence, though worthy of pursuit, can be explained as the result of hard work, good planning, persistence. It can be credited to the right type of personality or gifting. The impossible, however, cannot be explained by human effort or accounted for by a person's talents or training.

SUPERNATURAL POSSIBILITIES

The impossible is beyond our potential for excellence. It lives in the realm of the supernatural and operates in the lives of those who refuse to settle for what we could ask or think. It is according to the power that works in us. Simply put, it is not by our ability, but the ability of the One who lives in us. If we stop at excellence, we reduce the Gospel to a self-help philosophy and deny its power. With the Holy Spirit resident in our being, we have the privilege to explore and adventure in the realm of the impossible.

Growing up in the church, I often heard First Corinthians 2:9 preached referencing Heaven:

Eye has not seen, nor ear heard, nor have entered into the heart of man the things which God has prepared for those who love Him (1 Corinthians 2:9).

We can be sure that Heaven will hold things beyond our imagination, but this is not what Paul, by the inspiration of the Holy Spirit, is referring to. The next verse makes it clear that he is talking about the here and now:

But God has revealed them to us through His Spirit. For the Spirit searches all things, yes, the deep things of God (1 Corinthians 2:10).

There is revelation that awaits us in the Holy Spirit that we have yet to discover, things thought impossible in our present mind-set. There are experiences that are hanging in the atmosphere of Heaven, yet to be appropriated, that are impossible until they are made possible by the revelation of the One who lives in us. There are creative expressions that have not been revealed that will be experienced, diseases thought unconquerable that will be conquered, scientific impossibilities that will become reality, inventions yet unthought-of will come into being. All these impossibilities and much more, hidden in the heart of God, are there to be discovered by those who are filled with the Holy Spirit, pursuing excellence, and captivated by the impossible. They are hidden, in order to be found for, *"It is God's privilege to conceal things and the king's privilege to discover them"* (Prov. 25:2 NLT).

This is NIS on spiritual steroids.

ENDNOTE

1. *American Heritage Dictionary, Second College Edition*, s.v. excellence.

Chapter Twelve

Building God's Way

"I have found that sitting in a place where you have never sat before can be inspiring." —Dodie Smith

"Building program"—those might be two of the most dreaded words in a pastor's vocabulary, at least it was in mine. We needed to build a new sanctuary, and though I'd never led a church through that process, I had witnessed others going through it enough to discourage me. Many of my ministry colleagues had taken on the task, only to resign in complete exhaustion when the building was complete. The fundraising technique I had observed seemed more like a cheesy marketing scheme than the strategy of the Kingdom of God. I expected to hear an announcer say, "And for just $19.99 you also get..."

My lack of enthusiasm was encouraged by our church's history. The building of the original structures on our present site had left the church in such heavy debt that ministries were restricted and staff underpaid. The weight of the financial bondage affected everything in the church. Along with this difficulty, on three occasions in the past, architectural drawings had been commissioned and paid for. Each time, attempts were made to raise the funds to build a large sanctuary in order to complete the original plan for our campus. Every effort ended in frustration, discouragement, and wasted resources.

Searching for a New Model

Despite this history, the Lord was beginning to make it clear that He wanted the sanctuary built. Realizing this, Deborah and I, along with the church board, committed ourselves to see it happen God's way, completely free from the manipulation of human hands. We often wistfully wondered, "Is it possible that there is a place where a church building could be erected in a way that leaves the congregation free from debt and the fingerprints of man? And is it possible that Vacaville could be that place?" We moved forward with the hope in our heart that the answer was a divine yes. The journey became quite interesting.

In 1997, a couple of our staff pastors and I attended Tommy Barnett's annual Pastors' Conference in Phoenix, anxious to be exposed once again to Tommy's gigantic heart and infectious faith.

We listened intently as he presented the Dream Center, a new ministry his church was sponsoring in Los Angeles. The center would be led by Tommy's son Matthew, and promised to have a great impact on people bound by addiction and harmful lifestyles. I knew the Holy Spirit was prompting me to give to this important venture.

Deborah and I have always loved joyous, obedient giving, so hearing from God about an offering was nothing new. Following one of the sessions, I walked up on the hill behind the sanctuary they called Prayer Hill to hear what the Father had in mind.

AN AMAZING ANSWER

I heard these words: "All of it." It became immediately clear to me that God was talking about the money our church had put aside for the new sanctuary, a sum of $120,000. That was a lot of money to us, and it had taken several months to accumulate, but I knew I was hearing from God, and He was serious.

This divine appointment at Prayer Hill marked the beginning of a different era for me. I was called to function in the word of knowledge as God gave me instructions and tested my faith to a totally new level. I wasn't getting any direction that was even vaguely safe: either I was hearing the Holy Spirit or I wasn't. But He soon assured me that I wasn't walking alone, by using something personal to me to confirm this new path.

There on Prayer Hill and throughout the rest of the afternoon, one of my favorite hymns, "Great is Thy Faithfulness," echoed in my mind and heart. That night, as Tommy prepared to receive the offering and faith promises for the Dream Center, I gathered my courage and wrote a brief message on a pledge card. "$120,000.00—Tommy, please call me." I have never been more fearful in the midst of an act of faith as I was in that moment. Then just as I dropped the pledge card in the offering basket, the choir and orchestra broke into a chorus of "Great Is Thy Faithfulness." The memory of that moment would hold me in the place of faith during the testing months ahead.

Several weeks later, we presented a check for $120,000 to Tommy Barnett, and the Holy Spirit said to me, "Within a year, you'll be ready to begin building." I knew what that meant. As part of keeping the building project free from human manipulation, we felt strongly that we were to pay cash as we built. To do that, we needed to have $1,000,000 in the bank before we started the project. God definitely upped the ante when He asked me to believe that we would have that much in the bank within a year. It had taken us longer than that to raise the money we had just given away.

I have to admit, my faith was so weak that I didn't tell anyone what the Holy Spirit had promised, not even my wife. But God was faithful to give me a dream that would confirm His word.

The dream came early on a Sunday morning, a week after hearing the promise. There were two scenes in the dream. In the first, Deb was standing near the front of the sanctuary with her eyes closed, praying out loud. Lying on the floor in front of her was a woman with her head under a chair. In the second scene, I saw Deborah laying in a fetal position on the floor near the altar. In both pictures she was wearing a dress I had never seen before.

I got up and went to church early that morning to speak in a pre-service meeting; Deb wasn't dressed for church when I left the house. By the time I came into the first service, worship had already begun and Deb was waiting for me in the front row. She was wearing the exact dress I'd seen in my dream. Shocked, I leaned over to her and whispered, "When did you get that dress?" She thought I was upset about the dress, but I assured her I was only curious and would let her know why later.

During the prayer time at the end of the first service, I turned from the person I was praying with to see Deborah standing near the first row, praying with her eyes closed. She didn't realize that the lady she was praying for had fallen to the floor and lay there with her head under a chair. The picture was exactly as I had seen in the dream.

Following the second service, I was again praying with someone and this time turned to find Deb laying on the floor praying in a fetal position. It was then I heard the Father say into my spirit, "I gave you a dream and brought it to pass in the same day. I did that so that you would know that what you heard in your spirit about the building fund was my voice and that I intend to bring it to pass."

The Sunday following this dream I stood before the congregation and boldly told them what the Holy Spirit had said. This would be the last thing I would say publicly about the building project for several months as the Holy Spirit instructed me to remain silent. This was a strange way to raise funds.

Then one morning I was just waking up when I asked God how He was going to perform the promised miracle that would provide the funds we needed. He said, "I'll bring you a man." And he showed me a man walking into the church building. I couldn't see his face, but I noticed the pattern in the shirt he was wearing.

BIGGER AND BETTER THAN OUR DREAMS

The next Sunday, the Holy Spirit finally released me to talk about the new sanctuary and encourage the people to give. He was very clear that I was to tell them to mark the date as significant. Following the second service a man and his wife approached me to talk about the building fund. They revealed to me that they represented a foundation that looks for ways to bless the Kingdom and were interested in helping with our project.

When the man told me their foundation would match every dollar the church raised in the following year, I noticed he was wearing the shirt I'd seen in the vision. We would later learn that the man had started from home with a different shirt, but noticed he had spilled cologne on it and he went back into the house and put on the shirt the Holy Spirit had shown me.

You can imagine the renewed enthusiasm of the people when they heard of the matching funds. Everyone increased their giving and the building fund began to grow.

The date we handed the check to Tommy Barnett and heard God's promise was April 23, 1997. On April 21, 1998, we were $600,000 short of reaching our starting goal. Deb and I were in a hotel room in Pensacola, Florida, where we had traveled to see our daughter and attend services at Brownsville Assembly of God. We were expecting to receive the first matching funds from the foundation in the amount of $200,000 so I called the church office and asked if it had arrived. I was informed that no one had heard from the foundation and no funds had been deposited in our account. Concerned, I called the foundation and asked if there was a problem. The man told me there had been a slight glitch, but it had been worked out. He then said, "We have decided not to match what you have given, but rather to give an amount to you for you to match. I will deposit $600,000 into the church's bank tomorrow." To say I was stunned is a huge understatement.

Deb was in the bathroom putting on her makeup when I hung up the phone and loudly announced that the following day we would have $1,000,000 in the bank and we could start the building. I then threw myself on the bed and began to give thanks.

Deb excitedly asked, "What's the date?" I honestly had not made the connection, so I was a little aggravated that Deb was more concerned about the date than celebrating the victory. "Who cares about the date?" I responded. "I just want to give thanks that we can start the building." But she insisted, "What's the date today and when did we give the money to Tommy?" Then it struck me. We would have $1,000,000 one day shy of one year from the day God had promised we would have it.

There are many more stories of miraculous provision and Holy Spirit guided decisions than can be put in this chapter. It will need to be put in another book someday. But for now let me share the core choice that determined the course we took in building God's way and set the course for part of our corporate life message.

WISE WORDS

The defining moment came several years before the building project began. Deborah and I had just become the senior pastor of what is now The Mission. It was Christmas Eve and we were sitting around the table in our home eating clam chowder and crab cioppino. With us were our dear friends and mentors, Paul and Margaret Schoch, along with an 85-year-old pastor from England. We had the sense that we were sitting with the apostles.

At an unexpected moment, Paul turned to me and said, "David, your job is not to pastor this church, but to hear from the Holy Spirit and do what He tells you." The conversation continued on, but those words were all I could think about for the rest of the evening—really for the rest of my life.

I believe it was in that moment a new journey began, an adventure based on the mind-set that we would settle for nothing less than walking in daily fellowship with the Holy Spirit. It was a spiritual earthquake that shifted the landscape of my life and would do the same for our community of faith.

CHAPTER THIRTEEN

Never-the-less

"Who dares nothing, need hope for nothing."
—J.C.F. Von Schiller

I was sitting on the front row of the church as the ministry time was coming to a close. The speaker of the evening and one of our great friends, Ivan Tate, was praying over those that had come down to the altar area when he interrupted his prayer and gave an invitation that grabbed my attention in a personal way. "If you have wanted to bear children but have been unable to conceive, come to the front and I will pray for you." He went on to give testimony of others he had prayed for and later been able to have children.

Please understand, I was not interested in personally answering his call. Deborah and I love and enjoy our children and grandchildren and have no interest in conceiving any others. However, I was particularly interested to see how my daughter Amy and her husband Bryant were going to respond.

Several years ago, Amy was diagnosed with a condition that would not allow her body to conceive. The condition was not curable and the doctors gave her little hope of ever bearing a child. Though we understood this to be a fact, we were confident in God's ability to heal her and give them a child.

Over the years, Amy and Bryant have been prayed for many times. It seemed that everywhere they went they attracted people praying for those who could not conceive. They willingly presented themselves to be prayed for and continued to believe for a miracle. During those times, they would receive prophetic words from friends and prophets, all declaring that the time would come when they would conceive and Amy would give birth.

As time passed and the evidence grew that she would be barren, Amy continued to believe, but struggled with an increasing heartsickness as she watched her sisters-in-law and friends grow their families. And she continued to answer the invitations for prayer. I was curious though—would she come this time?

Three years prior to that Sunday night service with Ivan, Amy and Bryant decided to adopt a child, and through amazing circumstances they were offered a newborn baby girl they named Isabelle.

It was evident to all our family that she was a gift from the Father, and we could not love a child more than we do Isabelle. Amy and Bryant were very proud, contented, and thankful parents. But upon hearing Ivan's invitation, I wondered if they had given up on the prophetic words over their lives promising conception? Were they tired of putting themselves at risk of a letdown? Would Amy and Bryant be willing to test their faith and present themselves to the Father one more time? I'll tell you the rest of that story later in this chapter.

PETER, MAN OF CONTRADICTIONS

Simon Peter has to be one of the most fascinating characters in Scripture. He is a paradox in personality and character. On the one hand, he answers Jesus' question, *"Who do you say that I am?"* with astounding revelation, and on the other, responds to Jesus' declaration that He must go to Jerusalem and die with a remark that elicits Jesus's response, *"Get behind me Satan, you are more mindful of the things of man than of God"* (Matt. 16:15, Mark 8:29, Luke 9:20, Mark 8:33). He stands on the day of Pentecost and gives the opening sermon of the church age and then later three times declares, *"No, Lord"* when God commands him to eat unlawful food.

I love reading his stories and enjoy putting myself in his place and asking how I would respond if I had the same choice in the same context. What would I have said or done? When I do this little exercise, I find that I understand his responses better and appreciate the way he ultimately comes back to faith.

I was meditating this way one day while reading the story found in Luke 5 and discovered something I had not noticed before. The story takes place on the shores of Galilee. Peter and his fishing buddies are on the shore repairing and cleaning their nets following a fruitless, all-night fishing trip. A large group of people had gathered around the shoreline because Jesus is there and about to teach. Jesus turns to Peter and asks permission to use his boat as a platform from which to speak. After Jesus teaches, he tells Peter to do something that must have sounded like utter nonsense to Peter. He told him to take the boat away from the shore and throw his nets out for a catch.

If you put yourself in Peter's place you can understand the absurdity of Jesus' command. Peter was a professional fisherman. He knew the best time, the best places, and the best methods. He knew fishing. What Jesus was asking him to do was contrary to everything he understood about finding and catching fish. This itinerant preacher was telling him to do something that would be potentially embarrassing and put him at the risk of ridicule. His initial response was understandable: *"We have toiled all night and caught nothing"* (Luke 5:5). These were the facts.

CONTRADICTIONS IN YOUR LIFE

How many times have you believed for a miracle and not seen it happen? How many prophetic words over your life have yet to be fulfilled? How many years have you been standing on that promise of healing, or restoration of relationship, or salvation of that son or daughter and have not seen it come to pass?

You've done everything you know to do. You have fasted and prayed, claimed and declared. You've confessed and renounced every sin you have ever done along with a few others you heard about. You've forgiven everyone you can think of, including yourself, and asked forgiveness of every person you know, just in case. You've laid hands on yourself and performed personal deliverance. Standing in faith, you've answered every invitation for prayer on every occasion it has been offered. Still, the answer hasn't come, the sickness is still there, the relationship remains broken, the loved one has not returned to faith. You have fished all night and caught nothing. You can relate to Peter's hesitancy to do what Jesus has asked of him.

PETER'S BREAKTHROUGH

Now listen to the rest of Peter's response: *"Nevertheless at your word I will let down the net"* (Luke 5:5). The result was a catch too large to contain.

When I meditated on this story, I saw the word "nevertheless" in a different way. It was like a light shined on the word and it became three words—"Never the less."

Peter didn't have much faith in Jesus' suggestion to fish. This is obvious from his astonishment when he had to call in others to help him with the catch and he falls at Jesus' feet in repentance. But Peter did have a resolve, and that resolve was: "never the less, only the greater."

"Never the less" was not a casual "whatever" comment by Peter. I believe it came after a brief but intense internal battle that would not stand as an isolated instance in Peter's life. On this day, the word of the Lord was to go fishing; on another day, it would be to walk on water. Winning the battle on this day would lay groundwork for victory on the next.

I see Peter, in that brief moment of decision, dealing with several natural realities that stood in the way of a "never the less" response. These realities included: the facts as he knew them, his personal history that supported those facts, his lack of faith, the potential for failure, and the judgment of others. All of these are some of the same issues we face when responding to the word of the Lord. For Peter, and often for us, the easiest thing to do would have been and would be to give in to these realities —this would be the "less." But there was a resolution in the heart of Peter that sensed there must be something greater than these realities and he chose the greater—the word of Jesus.

The Facts Are a Low Level of Truth

The word of the Lord to us is greater than the facts of those places in our lives that have yet to have evident fruit. It is greater than our history and our puny faith. His promises, His commands, His declarations about our lives are all hanging out there ready to be fulfilled at His word. "Never the less" is a trigger point for the release of the supernatural through our lives in response to His word. It is a response of simple obedience, in the face of opposing forces, that unlocks the impossible.

"Never the less" is an NIS way of living. Not having followed inferior things demands of us a "never the less" response to life. It is a determination that the word of the Lord will not be subject to any opposition. The facts as we know them may scream it's impossible; never the less, we declare that God knows something we don't and His word is a higher level of truth. Our history may proclaim that it's never been done before; never the less, we put our hope in the one who can create anything out of nothing, and His word supersedes our history. Standing on His word may be fraught with potential failure and ridicule; never the less, we choose the pleasure of God over the fear of man, and His word cannot return empty. Even when we discover that our faith is puny and weak, "never the less" is a response that plugs our limited measure of faith into the one who is measureless, making our measure unlimited—above and beyond what we could ask or think.

Now, Back to Amy and Bryant

As I sat that Sunday night and waited to see if Amy would respond to the invitation, I wondered if she and Bryant would be willing to declare never the less, and one more time present themselves to the Father in response to His word. Would they keep presenting themselves until their faith became sight?

Watching with hopeful expectation, I saw several couples come down to the front of the room, but Amy and Bryant were not one of them. And then out of the corner of my eye, I saw my daughter walking down the aisle, and as she reached the front her husband joined her. One more time they put themselves in position for a miracle.

That event was around the time of Amy's birthday. This was significant since a couple of prophecies had linked a baby to her birthday. A month or so later, Amy was scheduled to have elective surgery and, upon arriving at the hospital, the nurse prepared her to go into the operating room. As she lay on the gurney wearing a surgical gown, head covering, and slippers, she heard the nurse exclaim from the adjoining room, "Oh, my God! She's pregnant." Upon hearing the nurse's excited cry, Amy looked around the room, wondering who it was she could be talking about.

It took her a moment to realize she was the only person in the room. The pregnancy must be hers. By this time, the doctor came into the room accompanied by the nurse, both of them with tentative looks on their faces, not knowing if this was good news or bad. The doctor stated, "Well, you won't be having surgery today, or for quite awhile, you're pregnant!"

Because of Bryant's travel schedule, it was easy for Bryant and Amy to identify the only possible date of conception—her birthday. Never the less, only the greater.

As I write the conclusion of this chapter, Deborah and I continue to sorrow over the loss of our daughter, but we are blessed to enjoy Amy's son, our seventh grandchild, a boy named Samuel David—A "greater" for sure!

CHAPTER FOURTEEN

Dreamers and Bards

"Imagination is more important than knowledge,
knowledge is limited." —Albert Einstein

At the start of the 2005 Potter's House, our training school for living naturally supernatural, Deborah and I were sitting with the first-year students sharing some of our life story, when a revelation dropped into my heart and a whole new adventure began. Deb was telling the story about our courtship and the day I proposed to her.

It was Christmas Day and we were traveling from her home in Moss Landing to my sister's house in Santa Cruz, where we were to meet my family for dinner. As we approached Watsonville, a small town about halfway to our destination, I tightly gripped the steering wheel of my Ford Mustang, stared straight ahead, and spoke the words I had rehearsed for days, "Deb, would you marry me?"

The silence was deadly. I waited as long as I could and then gave the disclaimer, "You don't have to answer me right now, you can think about it." Finally, after what seemed like an eternity, a small voice pierced the distance between her seat and mine, a gap that had become miles during the long silence, "Yes, of course I will."

Deb would later confess that her hesitation came partly from believing I was asking, "*If* I were to ask you to marry me, *would* you marry me?" She wasn't quite sure she wanted to respond at all to the question put that way. The other reason for her hesitation, however, came from her surprise that I was willing to give up my bachelorhood. She knew that since I was a young boy I dreamt of traveling around the nation in some kind of ministry and had several times spoken about it as if marriage would be an unwanted complication.

I had heard Deb share this story many times before and have always enjoyed the pleasure that the memory evoked. This time, however, it dawned on me that I was now living the dream of my youth. In that moment I realized that for nearly 24 years my dream had been shelved by the responsibilities of family and church, but not forgotten by God. He hid the dream in His heart, let it grow, then gave it back to me in a dimension greater than that 19-year-old youth could have imagined. I was not only traveling in ministry in the nation, but in the nations!

Caught Off-Guard

The revelation that God cared about the dreams of my childhood so caught me off-guard that I broke down in front of the students with uncontrollable emotion. They stared at me, probably wondering why this 35-year-old story would bring me to tears and second-guessing their decision to come to a school led by an overly emotional middle-aged man. Deb was perplexed and I was embarrassed, but the truth is I was devastated by the goodness of God.

Exploring God's Abundant Love

In the months following that embarrassing moment standing before the first-year students, we began to explore with our company of friends at The Mission the freedom to dream. One of the most significant moments in the evolution of our church took place when Deborah and I stood before the people and gave them permission to dream their own dreams.

Granting the church permission to dream has set us on a path of unlimited possibilities. Childhood dreams, crucified by the realities of life and the limiting words of significant adults, are being resurrected and breathed on by the Holy Spirit. Artistic expressions of many kinds are being discovered and released—photography, painting, writing, song composition, recording, and sculpting, to name a few. Businesses with a kingdom agenda are developing, and creative ways of ministering are being explored.

Latitude and Indulgence

The full potential of all this is yet to be seen. In fact the word "potential" is no longer adequate since it suggests that there is a ceiling, a limitation. This place of dreams is the territory of possible impossibilities.

We are beginning to discover that God was not kidding when He said through the Psalmist, *"Delight yourself in the LORD and He will give you the desires of your heart"* (Ps. 37:4 NIV). He wasn't talking about Heaven when He moved Paul to write:

> *Eye has not seen, nor ear heard, nor have entered into the heart of man the things which God has prepared for those who love Him* (1 Corinthians 2:9).

He loves to dream with us and use those dreams to reveal himself, bringing transformation.

One of the exciting fruits of developing this dream culture in the church is that people are joining together and encouraging each other's dreams. We call it a new way of "fighting with each other." People are finding ways to partner in their journeys, and as a result, we have discovered a fresh atmosphere of unity that resists an unhealthy competitive spirit. We are contending for unity by contending for the dreams of our friends.

Graham Cooke has prophesied that we are living in a time of latitude and indulgence. It's a time when God has granted us permission to explore our dreams with wide latitude and a time in which God wants to indulge Himself. We are finding this to be true and can sing with the Psalmist:

> *We were like those who dream. Then our mouth was filled with laughter, and our tongue with singing. Then they said among the nations, "The Lord has done great things*

for them." The Lord has done great things for us and we are glad (Psalm 126:1-3).

STORYTELLERS

The first time we met Graham, he prophesied that God was developing our church into a Gideon's 300 (Judg. 7:7). This was not good news to me; it sounded like reduction. Gideon's army went from 32,000 men to 300 and they were facing an army of 135,000. Gideon had lost over 99 percent of his fighting force. If the percentage of those that stayed in relation to those that left in Gideon's army was the same in our church, attendance on Sunday morning would only include my family—and not all of us at that.

It took awhile, but this prophecy eventually became a word of encouragement as the Holy Spirit began to talk to us about Gideon and the men God chose to face the enemy.

The people of Israel had been living under the oppression of the Midianites for seven years. Each year as the crops became ready for harvest, raiders would come and destroy them, along with all the livestock, leaving the country barren. Their fear was so great and the conditions so poor that they lived in the dens and caves of the mountain region. Even Gideon, this great man of valor, was hiding in a wine press, afraid to winnow the wheat out in the open.

All of this was about to change, and everyone in the nation would benefit from the victory. The 22,000 men that left Gideon's army because they were afraid and fearful would all enjoy the freedom purchased by the hand of the Lord. The men who were released to go home because of the way they drank would sit and eat the harvest and lamb chops that would no longer be destroyed by their enemy. Every man, woman, and child of Israel would take pleasure in the prosperity this battle would usher in.

We Want to Tell the Stories

But Gideon and these 300 men would not only benefit from the triumph over the Midianites, they would be the ones to tell the stories of things the others would only hear about. The 300 would be the ones sitting around the family dinner table or standing in the city gates describing the indescribable feeling of being in the middle of a miracle, while others could only wish they had been there.

Here at The Mission we have embraced our destiny to be a people like Gideon and his 300 men and decided to be the ones telling the stories—to be bards chronicling the great deeds of our God that we have witnessed and participated in. The miracles are happening and the stories are being told. We are determined that our life message will not be an echo.

Therefore...

One of my college professors would often say, "When you come across a 'therefore' you should always find out what it is there for." Our "therefore" is there for defining our decision to be a mission station and not a museum.

When I read the words of Jesus to Peter declaring that He would build His church and the gates of hell would not prevail against it, I find it impossible to imagine that He had in mind anything that resembles a museum (see Matt. 16:18).

A museum is defined by the *American Heritage Dictionary* as, "An institution for the acquisition, preservation, study, and exhibition of works of artistic, scientific, or historical value."

A museum is a place where things are collected, gathered, stored, and displayed in order for us to view, contemplate, gain knowledge and perspective, and to appreciate what has been. It reflects the culture and society that it represents, and displays its history. Its goal is to educate and inspire.

Transforming a Culture

All of this is good. I personally enjoy visiting museums and have been at times emotionally impacted as well as educated—but never transformed. In contrast, the goal of a mission station is not to reflect the culture but to transform it, not to display its history but to determine it.

The mission stations of the early history of California were far from museums. They were outposts of destiny. Their primary purpose was two-fold: they were to claim new territory for the nation of Spain and change the spiritual culture of the people in the region. Once established, missionaries would be sent out to plant a new mission, thereby expanding the territory and increasing their spiritual influence. This led to a system of missions all up-and-down the coast of California.

Though the mission system in California became corrupt and was used as a political tool by the Spanish government, the basic idea in its purest form illustrates the nature of the Kingdom of God, of which the Church is a part. Jesus said the Kingdom is like yeast that starts small but leavens the whole loaf of bread (see Luke 13:21). It invades the territory and changes the makeup or culture of the dough. This is what we believe Jesus had in mind when He made that declaration.

On our first trip to the United Kingdom, Graham took us to tour Warwick Castle. It was first established around 1000 A.D., and its original purpose was much like that of a mission. Its primary functions were warfare, expansion and protection, as well as farming for provision. A community developed around and in the shadow of what would become an impenetrable fortress. In all the centuries of warfare experienced by England, the walls of Warwick Castle were never breached.

Much later in its history, the castle lost its original purpose and became a place where the nobility and royalty came to play. It hosted parties and diversions for the rich and famous. It was not long before it became what it is today—a museum, a monument to its history, lost to its original destiny.

As we stood on the walls of that castle, we were convicted by how easily the Church has often followed the same pattern and become so unlike the destiny Jesus had in mind. We determined then that the church God planted us in as leaders would not walk down that inferior path, but by the grace of God would set its course to go from glory to glory, and ever increasing glory—to hear Jesus say when He looks at The Mission, "Now that's more like it."

THEREFORE...

We have decided that we are a mission station and not a museum.

We honor the past, live in the present, and keep our eyes on the future.

We focus on what could be, not on what is or has been.

We see past events—successes and failures—as stepping stones not stop signs.

We pursue learning in order to be transformed, not learning in order to know.

We are not limited to the four walls of our church building. Our influence is not restricted by location—not even the nations are out of bounds.

We are more concerned about how many we send out into the world than how many we convince to come into the building. The number of people we have or do not have in our building will not be the measure of who we are or the measure of our effectiveness.

We raise-up world changers—not tour guides. We train commandos, not committees.

We are people of engagement, not observation.

We are people of our destiny, not of our history.

Therefore...We are "The Mission."

CHAPTER FIFTEEN

The Currency of Encouragement

*"I can live for two months on a good
compliment."*—Mark Twain

She had said she would never do it, but the words I
overheard her speak into the telephone were words of
agreement, not resistance: "Yes, I'll come and speak at
your women's conference." Deborah's positive response surprised me, but what she said next shocked me: "But I will
only come if my husband can come and partner with me in
speaking." I'm not sure if we were honored or disappointed
when the woman on the other end of the line agreed.

Speaking at a women's conference was probably the last
thing either of us wanted to do. It was certainly not on our
dream list. However, the privilege of being with our new
friends in Sydney, Australia, David and Norell Crabtree,
along with a real sense that it was on God's dream list for us
to do, consoled us as we made the trek to that beautiful city
and gave ourselves to the privilege. It turned out to be one

of the great experiences of our ministry and led to personal breakthroughs for both Deborah and me.

Following the conference, we had the privilege of speaking at David and Norell's church, Dayspring, on Sunday morning. After the ministry time in the first service, a woman came to me and reached out her hand, indicating she wanted to put something in mine. As I extended my hand, she placed a U.S. penny on my palm and said unquestionably, "Here, this belongs to you. I found it on the floor." There was no uncertainty in her voice or doubt in her words. She knew it belonged to me because I was the only one, outside of Deborah, in the church that carried United States currency. I was identified by the currency I carried, and the currency I carried identified my homeland.

As I stared at that penny, it dawned on me that this is true about our lives. We carry a "currency" that identifies us, and the kingdom we represent. Those of the Kingdom of God have rivers of living water as currency flowing out of their hearts. Those rivers should be declaring our citizenship. The fruit of the Spirit is another identifying currency that should be easily recognized as we "spend" our lives in this world. The world should be able to say, "Here, this kindness belongs to you."

Encouragements Pedigree

One of the most powerful currencies we have is the currency of encouragement. As people of faith, we have the honor of being the most encouraging people on the planet because we belong to the most encouraging Father in the universe.

My hunger to hear the voice of the Holy Spirit multiplied when I realized that the primary language of the Holy Spirit is encouragement. Romans 8:16-17 says:

> *The Spirit himself bears witness with our spirit that we are children of God, and if children, then heirs—heirs of God and joint heirs with Christ* (Romans 8:16-17).

He is not about reminding us of our history—but rather, He is constantly declaring into our spirit our destiny. In fact, we have living in us the Holy Spirit, the one Jesus called the Comforter. The name means "one who comes along side" or one who is an encourager. Encouragement is a part of His very nature and is a characteristic of that living water that should be spilling out of our lives onto discouraged people.

When we speak a word of encouragement, we come into agreement with the character and message of the Holy Spirit. We participate in the very nature and ministry of the Spirit of God and we are authentic expressions of the One who lives in us when encouragement flows from our lives.

Encouragement has its roots in the heart of the Father, and as such, it releases a powerful anointing into the atmosphere and brings life to the hearer. That anointing has the power to break the hold of a toxic world on individuals who are trapped in a cycle of pessimism and negativity. Encouragement comes in the opposite spirit and challenges the enemy's favorite weapon—discouragement—giving us permission to hope.

The Power in the Telling

I will never forget the Sunday morning I announced my daughter Amy's miracle pregnancy to our community of believers. Many of those sitting in that room had been praying for her over the years and knew the importance of the event. When the testimony—a powerful form of encouragement—was given, people not only rejoiced for Bryant and Amy but those that had stopped believing in their own dreams suddenly began to believe again. Those that had come close to giving up on long-term situations that never seemed to change suddenly were hopeful, and prophetic words that were almost forgotten took on fresh consideration. Hope—the joyful anticipation of good—exploded in their hearts through a word of encouragement.

Do you realize that you have an anointing that is imparted through encouragement that benefits the spiritual progress of others and releases the favor of God? Take a fresh look at Paul's words in his letter to the Ephesians through the interpretation of the Amplified Bible:

> *Let no foul or polluting language, nor evil word nor unwholesome or worthless talk [ever] come out of your mouth, but only such [speech] as is **good and beneficial to the spiritual progress of others**, as is fitting to the need and the occasion, **that it may be a blessing and give grace (God's favor) to those who hear it*** (Ephesians 4:29 AMP, emphasis added).

There is a world full of people who are stalled in their growth and need the enabling power of grace to move on, and we can be the ones to impart it to them through our encouraging words. What a privilege this is, one that I have often missed out on, both in the giving and the receiving.

RECEIVING IS A GOOD THING

Receiving encouragement has not been one of my strong points. To take someone's encouragement to heart felt like I was being dishonoring to God, since He is the one that gives us all ability. What I have discovered, however, is that I was dishonoring Him and those that were trying to encourage me by rejecting the words He wanted to say to me through them. He was trying to benefit my spiritual progress and grace me with His favor, and I was seeing it as flattery. This is changing however, thanks to a few words spoken by my friend and associate Dan McCollam in a passing conversation he probably doesn't remember. He said, "The Lord told me I needed to give the same weight to a word of encouragement I give to a criticism."

The moment Dan spoke those words the Holy Spirit put me on a journey of discovery that led me to identify and repent of a mind-set that is not from the Kingdom of God. It is a mind-set that equates humility with putting one's self down and makes a virtue of low self-esteem. I have come to realize that putting one's self down is not humility—it is stupidity; and low self-esteem is a tool in the enemy's hand. This is an inferior way to live and leaves us living far below our privilege as Sons of God. Until we believe we are who the Father says we are, we will be stuck in our history and never get on to our destiny. I could never have embraced the call on my life as I do today if this mind-set had not been dismantled and replaced by the truth. Encouragement has become a great friend.

"Let another man praise you, and not your own mouth" is an instruction to allow others to praise you, not a prohibition to receiving praise (Prov. 27:2). I am not talking about flattery, but a word of praise that imparts grace at a time it is needed most.

Emailed Encouragement

At one of the lowest times of my ministry, I awakened on a Sunday morning and had no interest in going to church. I felt like I was living as the man in the old joke when his mom wakes him on Sunday morning and tells him to get ready for church. "I don't want to go to church. Those people don't like me and I'm not sure I like them," complains the man. His mom responded, "But son, you have to go. You're the pastor!"

Opposition to the direction the Holy Spirit was leading was strong among many in the church, and I learned the night before that a man I trusted had betrayed that trust. As I crawled out of bed early that morning, my back hurt as if a knife was sticking in it. The last thing I wanted to do was stand and speak to a divided congregation. It had become my habit on Sunday mornings to intentionally ignore my emails, since it was not unusual to get a critical or discouraging email from some disgruntled individual. Sundays were tough enough without having to deal with that. But on this morning, I decided to take a look and quickly became thankful that I did.

The email was from Jeff Domansky, a young man who grew up in the church and was passionately going after God. I was surprised to see his email address pop up, as he seldom contacted me personally. As I opened his email, my eyes quickly went to a sentence tucked among other words of encouragement: "I am proud that you are my pastor." Tears poured down my face, so much so that I could not continue to read, and when I recovered enough to finish the email, I felt like the knife was being withdrawn from my back and healing oil was being poured into the wound. Eight words, eight simple words put together to form a powerful expression of timely encouragement that imparted a grace into my life that has effect to this day.

His would not be the only encouraging words that would come my way over the next few transitional years. They would come from my family, from colleagues, from the community of believers I am privileged to journey with, even from strangers. Each one of them imparted a needed grace, demonstrated God's love for me, and released courage into my spirit, for to encourage is to give courage.

THE WORDS OF A CHILD

My granddaughter was ten years old when I was preparing to make a trip into the underground church in China. It was not my first time ministering in that culture so I was concerned when I began to feel some unusual apprehension about going. Fear was sitting at my door even as I tried to exercise faith. Samantha evidently heard me express my concern and spent time praying for me. On the day before I left, she gave me a handwritten note on a torn piece of yellow notebook paper. I write it here as she wrote it, including the misspellings: "Throw an iron fist at the face of feer and evryware els the devil appears—Samantha Crone."

That word of encouragement from the Father through my granddaughter infused into me a courage that I can't describe. That yellow piece of paper is now kept in my travel pouch and it goes with me everywhere I go.

Let me share a few ways we can engage the power of encouragement.

Living Present Future

One of the other ways that encouragement has impacted me personally is in the way it is manifested as we relate to each other, by speech and action, in light of our destiny and identity. Graham Cooke, a friend and colleague, has given us language to describe this kind of relationship—it is living "present future." Living present future is, in part, standing together in our present circumstances with our eyes on our prophetic calling and helping each other pull that identity and destiny into the now.

I am so thankful that I am surrounded by friends who refuse to let me stay in my history, and are always speaking to me about the way God sees me and the things that are in front of me. Calling up the best in another person through encouragement is the essence of New Testament prophecy, and has become a major core value of those at The Mission. It is not unusual to overhear someone reminding another of who God says they are and what He has declared of their future. It is not only usual, it is intentional.

"I AM" STATEMENTS

One of my favorite moments with our Potter's House students is listening to them read their "I am" statements at the year-end graduation. During the school year, the students select two or three of their most significant prophetic words and process them into a statement that is in agreement with who God says they are.

As they joyfully and with great confidence declare who they are in God, I often reflect on the way they saw themselves and their part in the Kingdom when they first entered the school. Many of them were filled with self-doubt, convinced of a poor self-image, and their sense of destiny was more fatalistic that fantastic. Yet on graduation day, these same students stand completely convinced that they are powerful children of the King with a future filled with His favor and supernatural possibilities.

A large part of this amazing transformation comes from the present future encouragement that is intentionally introduced into every session by the leadership of the school, along with many others who speak destiny and identity into the students' lives.

GREATER THAN GOOD FEELINGS

A simple "Thank you" and other expressions of kindness and appreciation are also powerful statements of encouragement. People are underappreciated in our society, and a word of thanks can open a new world to someone. Deborah has made it a habit when checking out at Wal-Mart to get in the line of an Indian woman from Fiji. She makes sure to look her in the eye and say thank you. One day Deb came to the checkout counter and the woman looked at her and said, "I remember you; you smile at me and look at me when you talk to me."

I recently came across an article on the Internet called, "Praise as Good as Cash to Brain," by Julie Steenhuysen.[1] She suggests that the brain's reward center is stimulated by receiving a compliment in the same way as when the person is given a cash reward. She referenced a study by Dr. Norihiro Sadato of the Japanese National Institute for Physiological Sciences in Okazaki, Japan, in which he studied 19 healthy people using functional magnetic resonance imaging, a brain-imaging technique.

Dr. Sadato studied brain activity in the reward-related area of the brain during two different experiments. In the first experiment, participants were given cash rewards when they chose the correct card during a gambling game. In the second experiment, the same reward center was monitored when the people were rewarded with a compliment from a stranger. In each experiment, the reward triggered activity in the reward-related area of the brain.

God created our brains to respond favorably to positive stimulation. We can release the power of encouragement by simply thanking someone today for what they mean to us, what we appreciate about them, or what they have done for someone else. Having a lifestyle of expressing thanks and performing random acts of kindness is a powerful NIS way to live.

GOD TALK

Talking about the goodness of God is a major source of encouragement. Instead of talking about the price of gas or the political turmoil, we can fill our conversations with the beauty of the Lord, his generosity and his faithfulness. One of the last verses in the Old Testament gives us this encouragement:

> *Then those who feared the LORD spoke with each other, and the LORD listened to what they said. In his presence, a scroll of remembrance was written to record the names of those who feared him and always thought about the honor of his name.*
>
> *"They will be my people..." says the LORD Almighty* (Malachi 3:16,17 NLT).

Imagine, the ears of the Creator of the universe are tuned to the words of those that speak and meditate on His goodness; He claims them as His own, and Heaven says "amen" in agreement. A question we may want to ask ourselves is this: which kingdom is coming into agreement with our speech, the kingdom of darkness or the Kingdom of Heaven? The wages of the first is death, and the gift of the latter is life.

SHOW AND TELL, TELL AND SHOW

A few weeks ago, Dano and I were in a small village in the interior of Fiji. It was a beautiful setting for a recently planted church of about 50 new believers. We had been asked to speak in their Sunday morning service by the pastor of the mother church, and after about an hour-and-a-half journey along a gravel road, we arrived at a carport-like covering in the midst of sugarcane fields. The people were exceptionally receptive as we began to share the goodness of God and remind them that the Gospel of the Kingdom is good news.

In illustrating the goodness of God, I related the story of a healing that we witnessed several years before when we prayed for a young deaf and mute boy in another part of Fiji. After sharing that story, we began praying for the sick, and a father brought his young son to us and through the translator told us the boy was both deaf and mute since birth. I turned to Dano and said, "Here we go again," and before I could move Dano jumped to his feet and tenderly placed his hands on the boy's ears and began to speak healing into his life.

After praying for several minutes, we asked the boy's father to ask the child if he could hear. The boy indicated that he was hearing something and we continued to pray. Then the father looked at his son and said in a quiet voice, "Say *Bula*"—a Fijian greeting that the boy had never heard before nor ever formed with his tongue. Dano and I along with those 50 other believers erupted in loud joy when the boy clearly and confidently said, "Bula." Speaking of the goodness of God had encouraged the faith of that father to believe that if God did it before, He was good enough to do it again.

TALKING ABOUT MIRACLES BUILDS FAITH

That brings me to another way to release the power of encouragement—the sharing of miraculous testimonies. You can't hang around Bill Johnson for any time at all without him sharing a story or two of a miraculous healing or a dynamic God encounter. Along with the story, he will invariably remind you that the testimony is a prophetic declaration of what God intends to do again. He really believes this!

Well, it has taken me awhile, but I have become a true believer. Testimonies are no longer the side dish of a good spiritual meal—they have become essential to the quality of my dining experience. Seldom, if ever, does a board or staff meeting begin without sharing stories of God's goodness demonstrated through divine connections, supernatural provisions, or miraculous healings. It is becoming more difficult to have a conversation that doesn't contain a testimony and an interesting thing that is happening; the more we tell the stories, the more there is to tell!

I was recently in a phone conversation with a friend in Australia when we stopped talking about the world and began to share stories of miracles that were happening around us. You would have thought we were sports junkies discussing the top ten plays from our favorite sports. We laughed, cried, and were even silenced in awe as we spoke of things thought impossible except for the miraculous power of God. I left that conversation and others like it full of faith, strong in courage, and expectant for what was ahead. My inner man was powerfully encouraged by the testimonies we shared.

I have watched the eyes of pastors laboring under the weight of a building program brighten, the faces of the discouraged come alive with hope, and the bodies of the weak strengthen just from hearing the stories of God's miraculous provision and healing. Cleddie Keith, a good friend of The Mission, says it this way: "The power is in the telling." He is so right.

SPREAD IT AROUND

Praising the character qualities of another, recognizing with appreciation the actions that demonstrate the Kingdom of God, living generously—all of these and more are other ways we can unleash the power of encouragement. Try them on for size; you'll be amazed at the results.

Encouragement is one of the currencies of the Kingdom of God. Let's spend it generously and maybe someday someone will come to us and say—"Here, this belongs to you." It is an NIS way of living.

ENDNOTE

1. Julie Steenhuysen, "Praise as Good as Cash to Brain," April 23, 2008, ABC News, http://abcnews.go.com/Technology/Story?id=4711656&page=1.

Chapter Sixteen

Conservative Christianity

"My dear McClellan: If you don't want to use the army, I should like to borrow it for a while. Yours respectfully, A. Lincoln."
—Letter to General McClellan in response
to the General's reticence to engage the enemy

I have one question and one declaration written on the inside cover of my Bible. The question is one that the Holy Spirit asked me on November 8, 2001. The declaration was my response one day later. The question came at a time I was fairly confident that I was sold out in my pursuit of God's presence and purpose. We had gone through a $3.8 million building program without borrowing any money; I spent my fiftieth birthday washing the feet of a persecuted apostolic leader in China; we were committed to going after the manifest presence of God no matter what the cost, and had already paid a large part of that cost. I really believed that I had pushed all my chips to the middle of the table.

179

Then came the question I knew was from the Holy Spirit: "What are you holding in reserve?" The question devastated me. Could it be possible that there were things I was holding in reserve, just in case? Had I hedged my bets, giving myself an out if things didn't work out? Had I made a conservative response to the call of God for intimacy with Him? The next 12 hours were painful ones of letting the Holy Spirit search my heart and reveal my motives.

I won't give you a list of things that the question and the subsequent searching revealed, but I will tell you that I awoke the next morning with a passionate declaration that is written next to that question in my Bible: "I don't want to die in a foxhole." Those words reflected my determination that if pursuing God was going to kill me, I wanted to die at full charge with nothing held back. This was not a commitment to "burn out for Jesus," but rather, a refusal to protect my life by withholding it from the battle.

Important Questions

I was challenged one day with this thought: "If one considers himself to be a conservative Christian, what is he or she conserving?" I realize that there is more than one definition of "conservative," but the thought wouldn't leave me. As I began to explore that question, several other questions came to mind. Is there anything written in Scripture or found in the character of God that would convince us that we were to be ones who conserve what He gives us? Just what about true Christianity is in any way conservative? Is there anything conservative about laying one's life down for another? Surely there was nothing held in reserve when the Father chose the sacrifice for our sin.

What is conservative about the love of God? The cross? Grace? Mercy? How can we speak conservatively about the incarnation—the willingness of Jesus to lay aside his position as God to become a man—the timeless and boundless One limiting Himself to time and space? All of these realities are radical, over-the-top, nothing-held-back expressions of a lavish and generous God.

Then there is the way Jesus described His church: *"I will build my church; and the gates of hell will not prevail against it"* (Matt. 16:18 KJV). This does not call up a calm pastoral scene of concession or negotiation, but rather a picture of uncompromising, militant, absolute victory. His church was not birthed on the day of Pentecost in conservatism, but in an experience of explosive power.

God in Whose Image?

What on Earth would lead us to believe that such an extravagant God would want to be represented by a conservative people and leave the expansion of His Kingdom to a cautious and restrained group of individuals? In the beginning, He created man in His image—why change that now? Could it be that Mark Twain was correct when he stated: "God created man in his image, and man, being a gentleman, returned the favor"?

Have we recreated God in our own conservative image? Have we redefined Christianity to the point that Paul or Peter would not recognize it?

In contemplating these questions, I have come to the conclusion that *conservative Christianity* is an oxymoron—a combination of words in which contradictory terms are combined. True Christianity is anything but conservative. It is following after and imitating the most radical person ever to walk on the planet—Jesus Christ.

A Radical Kingdom

The kingdom that Jesus represented and proclaimed is not a conservative kingdom. Jesus made this plain by using several similes that give us a picture of the outrageous nature of His Kingdom. He likened the Kingdom to a mustard seed that grows to *dominate the field* it is planted in; a merchant who *sells all that he has* in order to buy the pearl of great price; a treasure hidden in a field, a treasure so valuable that it is worth a man selling *all he has* in order to buy the *entire field*; leaven placed in a lump of dough, *so invasive* that it cannot remain hidden, but *permeates the entire lump* (Matt. 13:24-46, Luke 13:20,21). If these pictures are not enough to convince us that His Kingdom is nothing less than radical, Jesus adds this:

> *"From the days of John the Baptist until now, the kingdom of heaven has been **forcefully advancing**, and forceful men lay hold of it"* (Matthew 11:12 NIV, emphasis added).

I know in writing this chapter I risk offending some of my dear friends who consider themselves to be conservative Christians in the classical, traditional sense of the word. However, I find these friends to be far from conservative in their passion for Christ, their devotion to serving others, and their willingness to risk. I have learned much from their love of Scripture and obedience to its principles. Being true to the foundations of the faith is not what I am talking about here. I am speaking about those that have an anointing from the Holy One—which is every born-again believer—yet fail to recognize their privilege of releasing that anointing into their world for the expansion of the Kingdom of God. I am speaking about those that have "balanced" their life into neutral and become innocuous in their impact on the society around them.

The Kingdom of God is a kingdom of resource and resourcing. Everything we have been given is to be given away—love, grace, forgiveness, joy, provision, anointing.

Jesus stood one day and made a startling announcement and John recorded it this way:

"He who believes in Me, as the Scripture has said, out of his heart will flow rivers of living water." But this He spoke concerning the Spirit, whom those believing in Him would receive (John 7:38,39).

Every Christian has been given the person of the Holy Spirit and Jesus states that He is like rivers of living water. The key word in Jesus' statement is "flow." These rivers of living water in each of us are to flow out of us, not be stored inside of us. In the human body when things don't flow as they were designed, it is called constipation. Christians that do not release the flow of the dynamo called Holy Spirit through their lives are spiritually constipated. This makes for mean Christians—which is another oxymoron. No wonder some Christians look and act the way they do. They're trying to hold back the One who created the universe.

GIVE IT OR LOSE IT

Jesus made it very clear through a parable that holding back for ourselves what we have been given is not pleasing to the Father:

> *The ground of a certain rich man yielded plentifully. And he thought within himself, saying, "What shall I do, since I have no room to store my crops?" So he said, "I will do this: I will pull down my barns and build greater, and there I will store all my crops and my goods. And I will say to my soul, 'Soul, you have many goods laid up for many years; take your ease, eat, drink and be merry.'" But God said to him, "Fool! This night your soul will be required of you; then whose will those things be which you have provided?" So is he who lays up treasure for himself, and is not rich toward God* (Luke 12:16-21).

Notice all the personal pronouns: "I will store *my* crops and *my* goods;" "I will pull down *my* barns;" "I will say to *my* soul." At the heart of those who withhold what they have been given is the assumption of ownership. If we believe we own it, we mistakenly believe we can do with it what we will. What God brings to us and releases in our lives, our families, and our churches is not ours to own, only ours to steward. As stewards, we have the privilege of partnering with God in the distribution of Kingdom resources.

Bill Johnson, in his book *Dreaming with God*, makes the statement that, "We only get to keep what we give away." This revelation came to him when the Lord spoke to him saying, "What I am bringing into the house has to have a way of being released from the house, or it will die in the house."[1]

How many decaying resources are stinking up the house because we felt we needed to conserve them for our own use? More importantly, what has been left without resource because we chose to be conservative in our response to the Holy Spirit, believing the supply was limited? How much of our life has been taken from us because we tried to conserve it? Jesus said those who keep their life will lose it; those that lose their life will find it.

The superior things of life are lost through our conservatism.

Joash, the King of Israel, stood with victory over his enemies literally in his hands in the form of a quiver full of arrows. At the instruction of the prophet Elisha, he was to prophetically strike the ground with those arrows, proclaiming the total defeat of the Syrians. He responded with a half-hearted attempt—striking the ground only three times. The prophet's words are a warning for us today:

> *You should have struck five or six times; then you would have struck Syria till you had destroyed it! But now you will strike Syria only three times* (2 Kings 13:19).

Joash's cautious and restrained response produced only temporary victory. A conservative response to an invitation from the Holy Spirit will give us only a partial victory, and partial victory is partial defeat.

"I'm Not Going to Heaven in a Boat"

Several years ago, I was walking over a beautiful piece of property that was being developed by a dear friend of ours, Ivan Tate, as an orphanage for children in Guatemala. As

Ivan was describing his vision for the property and his love for orphans, I became lost in my own thoughts, thoughts I believe were directed by the Holy Spirit. I was thinking about the story of Peter walking on the water and realizing that even though he failed to stand strong and began to sink, he was the only one to get out of the boat. In the next moment, I had what I could only call a vision. Though the events in the vision took place over several minutes, it only took a few seconds in real time to be revealed.

I was in a boat heading toward a shoreline. I could see around me that there were many other boats scattered in front of me and along the horizon behind me, all heading the same direction. I was alone in my boat, as was the case with all the other boats. There were also people approaching the shore without a boat; they were walking on the water.

When my boat beached on the shore, the Father was standing there waiting for me with a big smile on His face. He greeted me by name and said He was so glad to see me, that He had been waiting for me and said I was worth the price He paid for my salvation. Then He got a quizzical look on His face and asked me this question: "David, what are you doing in that boat? I made you to walk on water."

I tried to give what seemed to be a reasonable response. "I had the responsibility of the church—they were counting on me. If I took too much risk, the people in the church wouldn't follow and I would look like a failure. There was my family to take care of, practical responsibilities to deal with. Others were encouraging me to play it safe; they said I was being prudent and wise staying in the boat."

As the Father patiently listened, my reasonable responses became less reasonable, more like hallow excuses. Then He spoke: "Come on David—what's the truth? Why did you stay in the boat?" I knew in that moment that I came in a boat because I had lived a conservative life.

His response broke my heart. "David, I was always with you—I told you I would never leave you; I gave you my Holy Spirit to remind you of this and to give you power to do works greater than the works of my Son. Now, before you step ashore I want you to think of this one thing: David—what could you have been if you had gotten out of the boat?"

The vision ended, and out of my spirit and my mouth erupted this declaration, "I am not going to Heaven in a boat!"

DEBORAH'S DREAM

Deborah had a similar dream a couple of years ago. She dreamed that she had entered Heaven and stood before the Lord. There, she noticed that there were many packages stacked up on the floor around Jesus' feet. They were wrapped as if they were prepared for shipping. Deborah asked the Lord what they were for and was shocked at His answer: "These were all the things I had prepared for you," He responded, "but you never put yourself in a position to need them—so they have remained here unused." Deborah awoke with a fresh resolve to live in such a way as to need and ask for everything God had for her.

Living a conservative Christian life is an inferior way to live and so contrary to the nature and character of Christ and His Kingdom.

UNRESTRAINED GENEROSITY

I have found it interesting, when reading through the gospels, that Jesus refuses to condemn lavish, extravagant, and even unrestrained, generosity. In fact, what the disciples called wasteful, Jesus called worship; what man would call unwise, Jesus often called great faith.

One day, Jesus was watching the offering being taken and what He saw so amazed Him that He had to turn to His disciples and draw their attention to it. What caught Jesus' attention was the offering of a poor widow—two pennies. The remarkable thing about this offering was that it was all she had. What amazes me is that we have no record of Jesus going after her and encouraging her to be wiser in her generosity, or of Him replacing her offering from His own purse. He simply praised her to His disciples for giving more than anyone else because she gave all.

WASTE OR WORSHIP?

On two separate occasions, a woman came to Jesus with an alabaster box filled with a very expensive oil. On one of those occasions, the woman poured the entire vial of oil on Jesus' head, and on the other, the woman used the oil to anoint His feet. In both of these stories, the oil was so valuable and the act of anointing so outrageous that it offended the conservative mind-set of the people who witnessed it. But Jesus' response to both of these women—approving their extravagance—silenced their complaints.

Matthew, when recording the anointing that took place in Simon the leper's home, states that the disciples were indignant and questioned, *"Why this waste?"* (Matt. 26:8). He then gives Jesus' response as one of not only approving the act, but declaring that her story of outrageous generosity would be told throughout history wherever the Gospel was preached.

Luke gives a similar account when recounting the anointing that took place in the Pharisee's house. A prostitute crashing a party at a Pharisee's house seems a bit humorous to me; however, you can be sure that it was not in the least bit funny to the Pharisee. It must have taken everything within him to control himself while witnessing a sinful woman coming into his house full of guests, weeping uncontrollably, allowing her tears to fall on his honored guest's feet, wiping her tears with her hair, and then having the audacity to kiss the man's feet.

On top of all that, he sees this woman pour expensive oil generously over Jesus' feet, oil acquired by means the Pharisee didn't even want to consider. I am astounded that he was able to keep his thoughts to himself, though Jesus had no problem discerning them. Jesus' response to this outrageous scene was to equate the woman's actions to honor given and love expressed, and He declared her forgiven. Conservative? I don't think so.

Radical Service

Let me share one last thought on this subject. Victoria, British Columbia, is a wonderful place to spend a wedding anniversary, as Deborah and I can testify. The beauty of the surroundings and the majesty of the British-style architecture have left a lasting impression on our memories. Little did we know that the most impacting moment would be when we found a small plague on the wall in the Parliament building memorializing those from Canada that gave their lives in the Korean Conflict.

Though it was honoring those that had sacrificed their life in battle, I was stunned by the way it described for me the radical nature of the authentic Christian. I found myself leaning against the wall with tears pouring down my face as I read it over several times. I put it here as antitheses to the conservative Christian life:

> Those whom this scroll commemorates were numbered among those, who, at the call of king and country, left all that was dear to them, endured hardness, faced danger, and finally passed out of the sight of men by the path of duty and self-sacrifice, giving up their own lives that others might live in freedom. Let those who come after see to it that these names be not forgotten.

Endnote

1. Bill Johnson, *Dreaming with God* (Shippensburg PA: Destiny Image Publishers Inc., 2006), p. 82.

CHAPTER SEVENTEEN

Personal Transformation

*"Life is change. Growth is optional.
Choose wisely."*—Karen Kaiser Clark

FACING MY FEARS

One of my personal struggles as a young man was living with a fear of failure. For most of my life I made decisions based on my ability to perform. If failure was a possibility, I would find a reason not to try. This way of dealing with the possibility of failure continued as I grew older, and it affected my total approach to life—including ministry. I got rather good at masking the true excuse for my decisions by using logic that sounded spiritually reasonable. In fact, I was so good at it that I usually failed to recognize it and often called the decisions I made wisdom and my actions acts of faith. The truth is that it was the wisdom of man and that my faith was captive to a huge calculator—one that wouldn't let me step into the realm of risk.

Years ago, I came across the following anonymous poem and I include it here as a humorous illustration of the inferior path I was traveling down. It is titled "Butt Prints in the Sand."

> One night I had a wondrous dream,
> One set of footprints there was seen,
> The footprints of my precious Lord,
> But mine were not along the shore.
>
> But then some strange prints appeared,
> And I asked the Lord, "What have we here?"
> Those prints are large and round and neat,
> "But Lord, they are too big for feet."
>
> "My child," He said in somber tones,
> "For miles I carried you along.
> I challenged you to walk in faith,
> But you refused and made me wait."
>
> "You disobeyed, you would not grow,
> The walk of faith, you would not know,
> So I got tired, I got fed up,
> And there I dropped you on your butt."
>
> "Because in life, there comes a time,
> When one must fight, and one must climb,
> When one must rise and take a stand,
> Or leave their butt prints in the sand."
>
> —Anonymous

Well, my time to fight, climb, rise, and stand had come. Choosing to live according to my life message would challenge my "safe" way of living and push me into a process of personal transformation. It was giving God permission to put me in circumstances that would strengthen and prove my resolve. The following are a few stories that illustrate this.

Fiji

We have been involved in ministry in the island nation of Fiji for many years and have more interesting stories than we can relate in this chapter. Our first Fiji story actually started when Deb and I were in England at a conference presented by Graham Cooke.

On a Friday night while we were gone, Talatala Philimoni Kama Waqa, who was at that time the pastor of the largest church in Fiji and the leader of a network of churches, attended a Friday night meeting at our church with his nephew. When we returned to Vacaville we had an opportunity to meet with them over lunch.

Upon returning home to Fiji, Pastor Waqa convinced the leaders of his church network that Deborah and I should come and be the main speakers at the next national church convention. He did this without ever hearing us preach! Later, when we asked him why he invited us, he said that they needed to hear from a pastor who would allow God to move in the way he had seen on that Friday night. He wanted me to bring Deborah because the Fijians had never seen a white woman dance before the Lord.

The invitation to minister in Fiji overwhelmed me with anxiety. This was way outside the boundaries of my carefully structured world. When Pastor Waqa called to ask me to go, my first response was to delay so I could find a good reason to say no. But something was changing in me, and before I could say "no" or "I'll get back to you," I said, "Yes."

Who Said That?

I was shocked. What had I done? I had spent 24 years of ministry taking the safe path at every fork in the road. Missions trips? Sure, I'd helped build buildings. But I'd turned down any invitation to speak, both in the States and abroad, telling myself that "my church needs me," or "there isn't enough money," or the ever-popular, "I have a check in my spirit." The truth? I was intimidated, afraid to try. But here I was volunteering to put myself in the position to fail. I was the most surprised man on the planet.

That first trip to Fiji was a whole different type of milestone in our journey. Deborah and I found ourselves being used in miraculous ways that honestly amazed us. It was in Fiji that we came to grips with the call on our lives to raise up a church that could make an eternal difference in the nations.

The unmistakable move of God in my heart put my fear where it belonged. I was becoming more afraid of disobeying God than of venturing out of my comfortable box.

A Dramatic Dream

We returned home from Fiji for just a week before we were to leave for Brazil, and in that week I had a dream. I was in the ocean. The water was calm and I wore something that looked and felt like a life vest. Although I could see nothing but water, I had a real sense of security. I heard the Lord say, "Do you want to be in the middle of my will?" I said, "Yes," as I floated contentedly.

The water became a little rougher and the question came again; and still I said, "Yes," more strongly than before. The waves became disturbingly larger: the same question, the same answer only with more intensity. Then, as a huge wake broke over me, the same question reverberated through the deluge of water, "Do you want to be in the middle of my will?" and I awoke loudly and passionately declaring, "Yes, more than anything." That resolve would be quickly tested.

OUR RESOLVE IS TESTED

We had been invited to go to Brazil as part of the support team for one of Randy Clark's healing crusades. Randy is very well-known and loved in Brazil because so many have been saved, healed, and delivered from demonic torment through his ministry. Tired of believing in healing and deliverance while seeing only a few healed or delivered we were anxious to watch, listen, and learn.

When we arrived at the airport, another new friend, Ricky Stivers, told us that Randy's flight had been delayed, and he wasn't going to be there that night. It was the first meeting of the crusade, and they expected about 4,000 people, every one of whom eagerly anticipated hearing from Randy Clark. Rick said to me, "I think you're supposed to speak tonight." I laughed, sure that he was joking.

Deb and I checked into the hotel and were then taken to the venue. About five minutes before it was time for the preaching, Rick leaned over, looked me in the eye, and said, "Are you ready?" Again, I had prepared to decline the offer in my usual way when something rose up inside, a strength I didn't even know was there, and I heard myself say, "Yes." This was getting to be a habit.

As I said "yes" the Holy Spirit spoke a few short sentences into my spirit. Those few words were all I had as I walked onto the platform. Remember, now, we're talking about David Crone, a pastor who usually worked on every sermon for hours, afraid to speak anything that hadn't been planned in detail.

An Explosive Response

I went to the microphone and delivered what the Holy Spirit had told me. The word was short but it wasn't sweet— in fact, it was quite strong. But people immediately began to flood the altar. Shocked by the response, I turned to the interpreter and asked, "Did you say what I said?" He responded confidently, "Yes, I said exactly what you said."

Then I asked Deborah to come to the platform. She delivered another brief but powerful word, and the rest of the audience came to the altar, where all Heaven broke loose.

This was, and still is, a defining moment in our lives, a moment where God showed us that He was in charge, and He wanted to use us in ways we had never imagined. There was no turning back.

This reminds me of an experience Deb and I had on an anniversary trip to Canada.

Our Anniversary Adventure

Deborah and I celebrated our twenty-fifth wedding anniversary by spending a few days in beautiful Victoria, British Columbia. The day we arrived I spotted a 1958 vintage Beaver pontoon plane tied to the dock across the street from our hotel. It was available for tourists to enjoy a bird's-eye view of the island. It seemed to me that it was a great way to celebrate our anniversary, so I excitedly said, "Let's go for a ride." Deb was not so thrilled, but she eventually agreed, and we arranged to go the next day.

We awoke to rather stormy skies but made our way to the plane anyway, thinking they would reschedule the flight. Much to Deb's chagrin (and my delight) they said we could go. So we climbed aboard and put on the headphones so we could hear each other. Deb sat in the back seat and I sat next to the pilot. Soon our plane skimmed out across the bay and into the air.

Just so you get the picture, a 1958 vintage Beaver is about the size of a 1958 Volkswagen. It's possible to touch both sides of the plane at the same time. As we gained altitude and headed over the island, the plane began to respond to a great deal of turbulence. The farther we went inland, the worse it became. We would later be told that we were in the air during the worst windstorm Victoria had experienced in over 30 years.

Deb was starting to get a bit nervous and I was even wondering if this was such a good idea when the pilot's voice came through our headphones. "Are you guys all right with this?" Deb's response was a great illustration of how our personal transformation was progressing and how our life message was coming into focus. She boldly replied, "I'm all right if you're all right." The captain's next statement said it all: "Well, we've already gone past the point of no return; the best plan is to stay on course." So we did, in more ways than one.

MARRIAGE IMPACT

I honestly would have told you that there was nothing inferior about our marriage. But the Holy Spirit knew better, and he was about to shift the very foundation of our marriage. He was not changing it; He was transforming it.

Deborah is a fantastic gardener: she mows the lawn, plants all the flowers and shrubs, and trims the hedges, too. She loves working with power tools and actually wants to receive such things as a chop saw or laser leveler for her birthday. Deb's an excellent interior designer who plasters walls and does professional grade faux finishes. Deborah is a great cook…a wonderful mother and grandmother…a terrific hostess. It's amazing.

In the old days of safe church, Deb's favorite way to serve the church was to stand watch at her post behind the information counter every Sunday, where she'd greet people until the singing started, and then slip into the service unnoticed. She usually sat on the back row so she could quickly return to the info counter for the next service. She was content to stay in the background resisting any attempts made to involve her publicly.

Deborah was first to have many Holy Spirit experiences, which was incredible in itself, since she'd always been so down-to-earth about all things spiritual. She was physically healed of several long-term physical problems—and that was just one result of an extended divine encounter with the Holy Spirit. Later she went to a conference and came home shaking violently from head to toe, and it lasted for hours. I watched in wonder. I was confused but certain that she, of all people, wasn't faking it. God was up to something, whether either of us understood it or not. I stood and watched, like a live lobster that didn't realize the cold water was gradually getting hotter.

HERE COME THE PROPHETS

Then there were the prophetic words that were spoken over us. At the beginning, we weren't even sure people could be called prophets in our time. Now we drew them like flies wherever God took us exploring. They would spend a long time talking to Deborah about what soon became a prophetic laundry list of promises.

The prophets would speak to Deb at length, and then almost always look at me and say, "You need her." Then they would walk away or turn to Deb and continue describing her prophetic destiny.

These people were not talking about the Deborah I'd known and loved since I was a teenager, and it took some adjustment. No, it required transformation. It wasn't that I wanted to retain a position of power in our marriage; it's just that it felt so uncomfortable and unfamiliar, like trying to write with my left hand. My wife's character was already superior, but if these unusual prophetic people were right, she was becoming, well, one of those unusual prophetic people.

In what seemed like two or three seconds, the prophecies started to come true. Deb was receiving amazing revelation and was now willing to share it publicly. She began to powerfully minister to tormented people, with life-giving results. It was as if all the gifts and the abundant anointing God had packed into her life were now being released.

Renewal Gets Real

Theoretically, I was thrilled. But practically, I was not a happy man. God was using what He was doing in Deb to challenge my comfort level, expose my hidden insecurities, and unveil my wrongly placed identity.

I was not enjoying the Father's way of transforming me. What had happened to my wife? In the past, she had always been the one waiting for me to finish ministering; now I was waiting for her. I spent hours preparing a sermon that barely kept the man on the fourth row awake; then she stepped up to give a two-minute word that brought Heaven down. "Hey," I wanted to shout, "I'm the Man of God here. Remember me? I'm the pastor. The prophets flock to her and walk away from me? You can hate me or love me, but don't ignore me!"

Deborah didn't seem to be much help at first. She was beginning to understand things about herself that had mystified her for years, and for the first time in her life she was free to be the woman God made her to be. In all the joy she was experiencing, Deb was perplexed as to why I was having a problem. In my soulish emotional state, her advice to me sounded like, "I can't help you, get over it." Although this sounded like no help at all, it was exactly what I needed to force me back to my identity in Christ.

Now, the description of our conflict may be slightly exaggerated—but only by a miniscule measure. This was a season of intense pressure for both of us. But as the psalmist David discovered, the place of our distress was also the place of our enlargement (see Ps. 4:1).

Deborah and I met as young children and became sweethearts as teenagers. We have always been each other's best friend. But for the first time in our relationship we had to learn how to fight so that both of us win. We had to learn how to fight with each other and for each other, giving of ourselves to each other in a radical love. The process was grueling—but worth it.

We've found our footing on higher ground, and no one is more proud of my wife than I am. We have both taken our place in the army and are no longer simply a part of the audience.

Chapter Eighteen

The Trap of Reputation

"It takes your enemy and your friend, working together to hurt you to the heart; the one to slander you and the other to get the news to you."—Mark Twain

*L*et me tell you a story of a humorous event that took place shortly after I became the senior leader of the church. This embarrassing moment would be used by the Holy Spirit in the years ahead to remind me to not take myself so seriously—no matter what other people think of me—good or bad.

Deborah and I, along with Amy, who was about 13 at the time, went shopping for clothes for our summer vacation. The cool, air-conditioned Wal-Mart was a welcomed break from the hot summer's day in Vacaville, with the outside temperatures reaching well over 100 degrees Fahrenheit. I am not much of a shopper, more like a hunter, so I quickly grabbed a pair of jean shorts and went into the changing room. As I came out of the dressing room to model my selection and get Deb's and Amy's approval, Deb handed me another pair and asked me to try them on also.

I don't know if it was the cool air or the euphoria over leaving for vacation, but without thinking, I unsnapped the shorts I had on and pushed them down to my knees before I realized I was standing in the middle of the men's department in Wal-Mart. When I looked up to see the startled look on Deb's face and the horrified expression on my daughter's, I started laughing so hard I couldn't pull my pants up. With one hand holding a pair of shorts and the other trying to keep the shorts I had on from hitting the floor, I eventually stumbled my way back into the dressing room and closed the door. It probably only took a few seconds, but it seemed much longer. I continued to laugh uncontrollably as all I could imagine was the headline in the newspaper: "Pastor flashes in Vacaville Wal-Mart." Fortunately, only my wife and daughter saw the show, and I believe Amy eventually recovered from the trauma of seeing her father undress in public, although I'm almost positive she is in Heaven watching the DVD of that event right now—I can almost hear her laughing.

Reputation

Reputation is what other people believe us to be. It may or may not be true. Reputation changes with performance and is at the whim of those that are observing and judging our behavior and the results of our actions. Authenticity is who we really are.

Solomon states that *"A good name is to be chosen rather than great riches..."* (Prov. 22:1) and *"A good name is better than precious ointment...*" (Eccl. 7:1). The phrase "a good name" does not speak of reputation, but of character. The *Jamieson, Fausset, and Brown Commentary* defines "a good name" this way: "A good name—Character; a godly mind and life; not mere reputation with man, but what a man is in the eyes of God, with whom the name and reality are one thing."[1]

Those that care more for their reputation than they do for living authentic lives exist on the edge of a razor. They must make decisions that compromise their character in order to keep their perceived life intact. Reputation at all cost requires compromise at any cost.

Saul's Decline

Saul was chosen by God to be the king of Israel. Reputation always comes with public office, and Saul's reputation was growing as he began to lead the nation. Saul takes under his wing a young man named David, who had just killed the giant Goliath. He sends David out to continue the war with the Philistines, and David grew in favor with the other men of war and in the sight of all the people. Our love for reputation is most often exposed when the reputation of others grows. So it was with Saul.

As Saul and David returned home from one of their battles with the Philistines, the people met them on the road with singing and dancing. I'm sure this was a familiar experience for Saul, as Israel's infatuation with their first king continued and the number of victories piled up. Though Saul had previously on two occasions demonstrated his willingness to compromise to save his reputation, compromises that cost him his royal lineage, this homecoming would be the turning point that would complete the destruction of Saul's authentic life.

As he and David returned to the sound of singing, the words of the women cut deep into Saul's ego: *"Saul has slain his thousands, and David his ten thousands"* (I Sam. 18:7). Saul was outraged, and from that day on he hated David and gave himself to a depressing spirit. The love of reputation had completed the degeneration from an anointed, chosen king to a vengeful, hateful, and selfish despot.

Joseph's Rise

When you are considered successful in the eyes of the world, you quickly get a reputation that draws a crowd of those who want to pull on your "wisdom." Just as quickly, that crowd will disappear when something happens that taints that reputation in those same eyes. Just ask Joseph.

Scripture points out that:

The LORD was with Joseph, and he was a successful man....And his master [Potiphar] saw that the LORD was with him and that the LORD made all he did to prosper in his hand....he made him overseer of his house, and all that he had he put under his authority (Genesis 39:2-4).

Because of the favor on Joseph's life, he was raised from being a slave to having full authority over the household of the captain of the Guard. As he served Potiphar, his reputation as a wise and successful man grew. Joseph, however, was about to find out how fragile a reputation really is. On one day, Joseph was considered a man to be sought after with a reputation for loyalty and integrity. The very next day, Joseph was in prison, being accused of adultery and disloyalty. It didn't matter that the accusation was false; his good reputation was lost.

In My Own Life...

I became the senior leader of The Mission after functioning at the church as an associate pastor for three years. At the time, there were many challenges that stood in the way of the church surviving, let alone succeeding. Financial crises, moral failure, theft, and opposition of various kinds plagued our momentum. As we faced these challenges, God was gracious to us and gave us courage, favor, and strategy.

Each victory increased my personal reputation for having wisdom and integrity—notice I said "reputation." As my reputation grew, others in the church community began to visit or call my office wanting my help with some of their difficult situations. People recognized me in the stores and made sure to say hello. I was asked to serve on more boards than I had time for or wanted to. All of that would change when God visited our church and turned our world rightside-up.

We were longing for revival to come to our church. We were hungry for God to come and meet us in a way that would change us. We wanted to see the miracles and the healings that you read about in the Book of Acts. God answered our prayer, but I soon learned that His coming would require choices that would not always be popular or understood.

Deborah and I made the willful decision that we would pastor the people the best we could, but we would not try to control the move of God. What we discovered was that when God comes in, He comes to take over, and the things I knew about being a pastor did little to settle the fears of some of the people. There is a reason you often read the encouragement, "Do not fear" in Scripture when God or an angel shows up—it can be a fearful experience.

RECONSTRUCTION IS MESSY

Several years ago, Deborah and I took on the challenge of building our own home. For many months I would head to the church office in my suit and Deb would go to the building site in overalls. After my time at the office I would join her and we would work until late in the night. One of the difficulties during that time was that we had to live with the chaos created by the building process. Our schedules, our living conditions, even the way we related to each other had to be adjusted on the run, putting pressure on every part of our lives.

This is a good picture of what was happening in the church. God was disorienting our lives in order to reorient them. This was an exciting time for many of us, but we found that not everyone could—or wanted to—live in the atmosphere of transition. They needed something more secure and safe, and we were anything but that.

As we yielded to the ownership of God in the church, amazing things began to happen. People were being set free, lives were being healed, and a fresh new love for Christ and His presence was born. At the same time, some people began to question whether they wanted to be associated with the church and our leadership. It was not uncommon for someone to come and tell me they knew that what was happening was for the most part from God, but they couldn't stay. As I mentioned in the introduction, a man's journey is both personal and communal. This is especially true in the life of a leader. My journey was not mine alone; it was being lived out in a community, and therefore, it was not only changing and impacting me, it had its influence on the church body.

The Cost

As people began to leave the church, my reputation and the reputation of the church became tainted. Some of those that left avoided me in public, and the invitations to sit on boards ceased. The phone calls and visits from those wanting advice stopped, and calls and visits from those wanting to give me advice began.

I needed advice and counsel, for I had never walked this road before. However, most of the counsel that came my way was to go back to being the church we were before God showed up. That wasn't possible for those of us who stayed; we were ruined for anything other than the manifest presence of Christ.

It was never more evident that I had lost my good reputation when a Christian leader in our community came to tell me she and her family were leaving the church and said, with tears in her eyes, "You are an embarrassment to the church community."

All of this was difficult for me to understand, for all I wanted and was pursuing was the thing I thought every other believer wanted—a transformational experience with the living God. I now had to choose between my reputation and my genuine pursuit of His presence, giving Him the right to come any way He wanted. It was no contest. Protecting my reputation was an inferior thing that could not stand in the face of the supernatural presence of Jesus.

CLEAR-HEADED BUT NOT COLD-HEARTED

The church community had to make this choice also. One of the major turning points in this decision came on a Sunday morning when the Holy Spirit disrupted every part of the service with His presence. The worship exploded. People were weeping while others were laughing. Bodies were lying all over the altar area and on the platform. When the volume of this holy chaos quieted down, Deborah, sensing a conflict among some, picked up a microphone and made a statement that became a line in the sand for years to come: "We may not be able to explain everything that happens," she calmly said. Then with deliberate conviction she stated, "But we will no longer apologize for what the Holy Spirit is serving."

This was not a painless, cold-hearted experience. Any leader that tells you they are not affected by what people think of them is denying reality. The issue is not *if* they are affected, but in what way have they allowed themselves to be affected. It is a matter of choice. You either let the criticism hurt you, produce bitterness and stop you, or you let it harness you to your destiny. This is what Joseph did.

Following the betrayal of Joseph by Potiphar's wife, we find Joseph with a ruined reputation in the prison where the king's prisoners were confined. This was a moment of decision. Would Joseph remain authentic to the man he was, or would he give in to hurt and eventual bitterness? The favor of the Lord awaited his decision. He chose NIS and went on to claim his destiny.

Right Foundation

Believe me, as a public figure, dealing with the up and down seasons of good reputation and lost reputation is like riding a roller coaster. But it's a ride we don't have to get on when our identity is in our relationship with the Father and not in our reputation. Jesus is our perfect example:

> *Let this mind be in you which was also in Christ Jesus, who, being in the form of God, did not consider it robbery to be equal with God, but made Himself of no reputation, taking the form of a bondservant, and coming in the likeness of men. And being found in appearance as a man, He humbled Himself and became obedient to the point of death, even the death of the cross. Therefore God also has highly exalted Him* (Philippians 2:5-9).

Jesus willingly laid aside the highest possible reputation and took on the shame of the Cross, having his identity secure in the Father. In choosing humility and obedience, He put His destiny in the Father's hands and received the favor of promotion.

Our reputation may be in the hands of others, but our destiny is in the hands of God. Reputation, or destiny? The favor of the Lord awaits our decision.

A GREAT GIFT

The loss of my reputation has been one of the greatest gifts God has given me. In some ways, it has been the making of me, as every place of sacrifice has became a point of greater resolve. For that I thank God, the friends that stayed close, and even those that couldn't.

I wouldn't change what God has done in me or the church for any level of man's approval. It is not that I don't appreciate it; it just isn't the point of my life. My pursuit remains the same—the manifest presence of Jesus.

ENDNOTE

1. *Jamieson, Fausset and Brown Commentary* on Ecclesiastes 7:1, Electronc Database. Copyright ©1997, 2003 by Biblesoft, Inc.

CHAPTER NINETEEN

Resurrection

*"Only those who will risk going too far can
possibly find out how far one can go."*—T.S. Elliot

L iving out one's life message does not always leave us
with easy choices or lead down convenient paths. On
the contrary, it usually puts us on the road less traveled. I don't know that I fully understood this when I adopted the "not following inferior things" as language for my
life message. It is absolutely clear to me now.

Deb and I arrived home from the hospital on the day of
Amy's death devastated and numb. We were living our worst
nightmare. It seemed so unreal, yet the pain in our chest and
the sight of the empty chair where Amy had slept while recovering from surgery screamed through our fog that it was
true. Amy was gone and not coming back.

As a pastor, I had helped many people through those first
few hours following the loss of a loved one, but I didn't know

how to help myself or give comfort to Deborah. So, mostly we just hung on to each other and cried.

I don't remember exactly when, but at some point during those hours of agony, a resolve crept into my thoughts and I picked up the phone and called Graham Cooke. Upon leaving the hospital I had asked Graham and Bob Book to handle the arrangements for the Sunday morning service at The Mission the next day.

I was now calling Graham to ask another favor. When he answered the phone I heard myself say, *"Graham, we want you to stand with us and pray for Amy's resurrection."* He didn't sound shocked but asked a question that, at the moment, I didn't know how to answer. "What do you want us to do?"

"I don't know," I answered. I realized that I had just thrown down the gauntlet and there was no turning back. This was certainly a road I had not been down before. "Just let the people know tomorrow that we are praying for Amy to be resurrected and we invite them to join us." Graham agreed with enthusiasm and we ended the conversation.

The next morning we stayed home with our family and gave each other comfort. At The Mission, however, there was a different story unfolding. Later in this chapter I will let Graham describe the event in his own words. But for now, let me just say that the community at The Mission took on the challenge with great faith and enthusiasm. This was a fight they were up to.

By Sunday afternoon, the word had gone out literally around the world. Bill Johnson and Kris Vallotton from Redding were the first to call and join their churches with ours in the battle for resurrection. Then the troops from various places in the world began to report in and the army continued to grow. Churches and friends from all over the United States; Australia; China; Hungary; Denmark; Fiji; Philippines; India, and England joined their prayer with ours in agreement to do what Jesus told us to do: "Raise the dead."

We, at The Mission, didn't know a lot about raising the dead. We had never done this before. But this fact didn't discourage us; it just gave us a sense of anticipation that we could be the ones to witness the first of many. What we did know from hearing stories of those who had experience raising the dead, was that to be effective we needed to get our hands on Amy's body. This would prove to be difficult because the coroner's office was holding her body in preparation for a required autopsy and would not allow me to see or touch it.

However, this roadblock didn't stop those at The Mission from their mission. Christopher, a friend and medical doctor, was able to get permission to see Amy and spent some time singing and worshiping over her body. Several people began holding a vigil outside the coroner's office praying for resurrection. During this time I was speaking to officials trying to get permission to see Amy before the autopsy.

On the evening before the autopsy was scheduled, I was able to reach an officer that was willing to help me. He agreed to hold off the autopsy until later in the day so that I could at least come into the building and pray. I asked Dan McCollam to come with me.

Dan and I arrived to see 15 or so people from The Mission standing outside the building praying. After we greeted them, I knocked on the door and a young man let us into a waiting area. He proceeded to say that only I could go in and on top of that I would only be allowed to go into the room next to the room where Amy's body was held.

I accepted the conditions, left Dano in the waiting area, and entered the assigned room. I laid my hands on the wall I believed to be the adjoining wall to Amy's room and began to command life. After about 20 minutes the young man returned and apologized that he needed me to leave. I was reluctant, but knew if I stayed too long the officer may get into trouble. As I started to leave I asked him one more favor. "Officer, will you please go to my daughter's body and check her vitals?" He looked at me with compassion and said, "Sir, she has no vital signs to check."

My response surprised even me, "I know she didn't before I prayed, but will you humor this father that has lost his only daughter and please check?" He said he would and I went into the waiting room and stood in anticipation with Dano. I will never forget the look of compassion on the face of the officer as he came back into the room, and with tears filling his eyes said, "I'm sorry, there is no change." I thanked him for his kindness and we walked out to give the report to the team outside. The autopsy took place later that day. The conclusion from the autopsy was that Amy's death was the result of a massive blood clot lodged in the heart.

In spite of the fact that the autopsy had already taken place, we were not ready to give up. After Amy was taken to the mortuary I spoke with Bridget, the director, and asked if she would prepare the body so that I could come and spend an hour or so and pray over it before she sealed it in the coffin. Graciously, Bridget accommodated my request and she and her staff prepared the body and placed it in a private room.

My father, Dano, Bob Book, and Ivan Tate, a dear friend that had come to be with us during this time, and myself met at the mortuary and made our way to the room where Amy's body laid. Many others from The Mission had also gathered to stand with us. They were willing to stand outside and pray, but the day was so hot I asked Bridget if it was all right if they came in and prayed in the chapel. Again Bridget was very helpful and the crowd entered the chapel and began to pray and worship.

We did everything we knew to do. Bill Johnson had told me that in Mozambique they have seen hundreds of resurrections and that they have learned to pray over the feet first. If, within 15 minutes the feet begin to get warm they know they will have a resurrection and they continue to pray. If this does not happen, they know they will most likely not get a resurrection, no matter how long they pray.

We took this strategy to heart and began to pray over her feet. We commanded her to live, declared life over her body, and after nearly 30 minutes we knew Amy was not coming back. I asked everyone to leave the room and I sat in a chair next to Amy's body with my hand on her arm and had my last fatherly chat with my daughter.

What I am about to share may not fit your theology. It is offered here as my experience and perspective. I also share it as an encouragement to those that have chosen to pursue everything that Jesus gave us authority to do.

I am very confident that as we prayed over Amy's body we opened the portal for her to come back, but she chose not to. It was not a selfish choice; she just knew something we didn't know.

The morning I was preparing to go to the mortuary I believe the Lord said to me, "She will make the choice." I instantly recalled the story of my grandmother that my mother had reminded me of the night before. My grandmother raised nine children with little or no help from my grandfather. When all the children were still home and fairly young she became very ill and died lying on her bed with her children all around her. She found herself walking with Jesus in what she believed to be Heaven. As they were walking she began to hear her children crying with sorrow over her death. She looked back at the sound and Jesus stopped and said to her, "You can go back if you want to." God was giving her a choice, stay or go back. My grandmother chose to go back and raise her children, and it wasn't until all had received Christ and been baptized in the Holy Spirit that she went to be with the Lord.

Just before I went out the door to get in the car, Deb came back from her morning walk and it was obvious that she had had a revelation while on her trek. She said, "Dave, I fully support what you are doing today and will be praying that Amy is resurrected. But I need to tell you that the Lord told me that Amy knows something we don't know and the choice to come back will be hers." I knew this was the word of the Lord.

While we were in the room praying over Amy's body there was a young woman, Sierra, in the chapel sitting with her father. Several days before, Sierra had a vision in which she went to Heaven and spent some time with Amy. In the vision Sierra kept telling Amy that they both needed to go back to earth because they had important things to do. Amy seemed to not really respond but when Sierra came out of the vision she assumed that Amy would choose to come back.

Now, sitting in that chapel at the mortuary praying for Amy's resurrection, Sierra was again beginning to have a similar experience. Her dad noticed the look on her face and asked her if she was all right. Sierra told her dad that every time she thought of Amy she was right back in Heaven talking to her and no matter how much she pleaded for her to return, Amy just looked at her with an expression that said, "You just don't understand."

Amy's choice was to stay. What she knew that influenced that choice is only conjecture, but I am sure that it was something in the heart of the Father that drew her away from Earth and farther into Heaven.

Below is a blog that Graham Cooke wrote and released on his Website July 2, 2009. He has given permission for it to be printed here in hopes it will encourage the reader.

SAD, BUT ODDLY TRIUMPHANT: AN ANNOUNCEMENT.

Just a normal day. Saturday, eating lunch, watching New Zealand beat the French at rugby. My cell rings and tragedy comes through the airwaves. Amy Crone, daughter of my good friend and senior team leader David…has had a cardiac arrest and passed away.

Scrambling to the hospital. Theresa and I join with a small group of family and Amy's friends in the Emergency Room. My daughter Sophie, her friend

Kellie who works for me in Brilliant Book House, both come for tearful hugs. We are all shattered. Amy? Funny, creative, life of the party, mother of two—Amy...gone?

I stepped into the room where Amy lay. Deborah, her mom, is stretched out over the bed sobbing. David sitting head bowed at his daughter's feet. Mark and Tammy, good friends giving stellar support. We prayed, touched, stayed connected till the Coroner came and took the lovely girl away.

David and Deborah emerged, shell-shocked. They thanked and hugged everyone. I half expected David to say to me, "Is there anything you need? Anything I can help you with?" Typically the way most conversations ended with Dave. Watching the two of them walk across the parking lot holding hands is one of the most gut wrenching things I have ever seen.

Just a little later my cell phone rings. "We want you to stand with us and pray for Amy's resurrection." Absolutely, no problem. I'm on it. I can't remember what I actually said to my friend but I had never wanted a fight more than I wanted this one. Another wonderful friend Bob Book our worship leader at the Mission and our wives Theresa and Barbara met that evening to plan the Sunday morning gathering at the Mission.

The Crone family were gathering too and would do battle at the family home the next morning. Not wanting to be a distraction or a focus for grief and shock they chose their site of battle sensibly. Word went out all over the world. Our great friends at Bethel, Redding, Bill and Beni Johnson, swung everything behind their love for David and Deborah. People from all over the States and many countries united to pray.

That Sunday morning at The Mission will live long in my memory. I have never seen a spirit of unity manifest itself with such hunger and open delight. The worship was astonishing. The truest and best celebration of the wonder of Jesus. We exalted in the Lord our God. In worship we take what we know to be true of God in our experience and we stand in that place to rejoice, praise and offer thanks as an expression of our confidence in the goodness of God.

Lamentation is the highest form of praise that exists on earth. It is unique to earth. Heaven cannot copy it because there are no tears or sorrow in Heaven. Lamentation allows us to do something that Heaven cannot...worship the Lord when we are in a place of utmost distress.

Lamentation carries with it a "though" and a "yet" [Habakkuk 3:17-19; Job 13:15]. "Though" we are in a place of critical distress, where we are burdened and saddened beyond our strength to bear..."yet, we will exalt in the Lord.

To exalt means to be delighted, full of elation, in high spirits, jubilant, overjoyed, in celebration. God does not ask us to put aside our grief or our burden. He asks us to make it an offering. To step into the place of His Majesty and Beauty and bring it with us. Use it. There is never a good enough reason not to rejoice. Lamentation allows us to step into a place in the Father's affection where our tears mingle with adoration and He has first place ahead of our suffering. This is where worship enters the realm of glory.

As a spiritual community we are learning about, living under an open heaven, being made in His image, doing the things that Jesus did, living from Heaven to Earth. We are learning, growing and developing in the practice of, "on earth as it is in Heaven." Not experts by any means but in passionate pursuit of real Christianity.

It felt to me that we were under observation by a great cloud of witnesses. At one point we broke through into Heaven. Hundreds of people in delight. One heart, mind, voice and spirit...and our worship massively escalated. We joined in with Heaven. The sound was incredible. Half of our main band was out of town. We had cancelled the band for the day. All we had was Bob on vocals/acoustic, Byron on piano, and Ned playing a djembe! Suddenly, collectively, we were embracing a sound we had never heard before. It lasted for moments and then faded leaving us stunned, astounded and with enlarged hearts.

I shared briefly from John 11 and Mark 5...the stories of Lazarus and Jairus' daughter. Jesus spoke of death as a form of sleep from which people could be awakened. At The Mission we fully believe in all that God is for us and all that He can do. We rejoice in His goodness and we stand firm in His power and intention. As a people we are learning to stand in the place of devastation, degradation and despair as we bring the Goodness and the Kindness of God to a hurting world. Our desire is to bring Heaven to Earth with miracles, signs and wonders. We want the authority of the Lord of Life; therefore, we are choosing to fight every circumstance...joyfully.

We prayed as one heart, we commanded life to return with one voice. In football terms we left everything out there. Father's Day, how appropriate. Over the next few days, we gathered in small groups to continue the joyful proclamation of resurrection power.

Amy never came back to us. Dear, sweet, fun loving, zany, irreverent (she disliked organized religion/churchianity), Amy never returned from the place of delight.

The funeral was outrageous. Typical of the Crone family. It was a masterpiece of prophetic pioneering spirit. They set a whole new trend in graveside committals. No memorial church service, Amy would hate that. Instead a small number of family and friends met at the cemetery. We were all instructed to be dressed casually. Lots of jeans, bright colors, no formal wear. Two stretch limos pulled up and out popped the Crone family. A lone piper played Amazing Grace as they pulled two ice chests out of the trunk.

We gathered around Amy's coffin as David and Deborah spoke movingly of Amy's life. Lots of laughter and tears as people told story after story of this irrepressible young woman whose passion for God and life could never be dampened no matter how hard life became for her. We hooted with laughter and blinked away tears at the same moment. We were all given pink flowers to hold (thanks Amy) and spread over the coffin in last goodbyes.

Champagne and cider came out of the chests as we toasted the life of a loyal, sassy, individualist, free spirit who no doubt is teaching King David how to really dance before the Lord. Bill Johnson gave a short and moving address on the importance of mourning properly…to let both joy and sadness move in you…to suppress neither because that's harmful, but always let joy have the last word each day. He exhorted and encouraged us to be true to who God is and to contend always for Life. Amen to that.

The next day, our core leaders, Bob Book, Dan Mc-Collam and myself met with David and Deborah to plan the next Sunday gathering. More laughter, more tears, great cookies.

The sanctuary was full on Sunday. People came from all over the world to celebrate Amy's life. Moving, happy, sad, delightful…it was all that. Great rejoicing. Great family. Great community. Great Oneness.

We never got the resurrection that we fought for. Does that means we step back from what we believe? Do we now occupy a lesser place of no risk and maximum safety? Or do we step up, freshly determined to see:

Your Kingdom come, your will be done?

We are the belief that never goes away. We plan to weary the enemy by being ever-present with Jesus. Our ongoing joy and passion for God's real kingdom will eventually wear the enemy down. God did not take Amy; she was stolen from us and now we will make the enemy pay.

Our faith statement is found in Daniel 3:13-18. It is the story of three friends in Babylon who were ordered to worship a statue of the king or face a grim death. Their answer was an in-your-face declaration:

Our God whom we serve is able to deliver us from the furnace of blazing fire, and save us from your hand. **But even if He does not,** *let it be known to you O King, that we are not going to serve your gods or worship your golden image.*

It's called a pre-determined response. They knew the consequences of their decision before they had an audience with the king. No matter what it costs they were not backing down from what they believed. It was a wholehearted acknowledgement of who they were as Hebrews.

As a community this tragedy has united us and defined who we are going to be. It has called us up to a new place...brought ascension in the Spirit. We will go after:

Heaven on Earth

Being made in His image

As He is, so are we in this world

Greater things shall we do

We will go after the Glory of God. We will embrace His Nature, His love, Mercy, Grace, Kindness and Joy. We will choose to view our life through the eyes of His Goodness. We will go after Resurrection, Healing, Miracles, Power and Abundance until we see it, we apprehend it, and it becomes a normal occurrence. We want this fight!

We are in the process of making new decisions that define us as a community. We are not going back.

—Graham Cooke

We didn't get the resurrection of Amy we fought for, but I know someday we will raise the dead. I also know that not being willing to follow an inferior path has made us stronger, closer as a community, and more authentic as those who call themselves "believers."

As for Deborah and me, we are focused on a greater reality. The fact is Amy is no longer with us and our hearts are marked with that reality for the remainder of our lives. However, Amy lives, hanging out with the Father, standing with the great cloud of witnesses cheering us on and awaiting our reunion. This is the greater reality that is superior to the present facts.

A SPECIAL NOTE

It is now ten months after Amy moved to Heaven and several months since I wrote this chapter and sent it to the publisher. Since then, the power of Jesus has resurrected two people from the dead. I will share the short version of the stories with you.

The first resurrection was a five-year-old girl connected to our ministry in the Philippines. She was under water for 20 minutes and had no vital signs for over an hour. The people around her did not give up and continued to pray life over her body even as the doctor told them there was nothing he could do. As they prayed, she suddenly recovered completely and is a perfectly healthy five-year-old. Her name is Alpha Grace, and I had the privilege of embracing her father and celebrating his daughter's life. He is one of our students in the School of the Supernatural in the Philippines.

The second resurrection took place just a few days before Easter, here in our city of Vacaville. Chad is a 31-year-old married man with four children. His wife was awakened in the early morning by the noise of Chad trying to breathe. The paramedics came and tried to revive him and declared that he was dead for 23 minutes before they could get his heart to beat again. He was put on life support and the family faced the decision of when to withdraw that support. They and the other Christians of our city chose instead to declare life and believe God for a miracle. By the third day, Chad was responding, and by the end of the week, he was sitting up talking with family and declaring the goodness of God. I take personal joy in the fact that Chad had been a friend of Amy.

Yeah, God!

CHAPTER TWENTY

The Ultimate Pursuit

"It is not mere words that nourish the soul, but God himself…"—A.W. Tozer

his chapter is an "in case I haven't said it or you haven't heard it" chapter. There must be no mistake as to what the ultimate purpose of NIS is in my life. Simply stated, it is for the pursuit of Christ Himself. There is no higher calling; there is no greater quest. It is as Paul states:

> *I gave up all that inferior stuff so I could know Christ personally, experience his resurrection power, be a partner in his suffering, and go all the way with him to death itself* (Philippians 3:10 MSG).

He is the ultimate prize, and He has been my pursuit from the earliest moments when God first began to reveal Himself to me when I was a child. Relationship with Him has continued to be the growing passion of my life.

For more than 20 years of my pastoral ministry, I have served as the primary speaking voice in the churches I have been connected with. This means that every Christmas a Christmas message is expected. That's 20-plus opportunities to discover something unique and wonderful about the incarnation. This last Christmas season, knowing that sermon preparation can be a trap of sharing truth that has not been personally adopted, leading to religious form, I wanted to explore some things in my own heart about the coming of Jesus apart from preparing to share with the congregation. I began by asking some questions of the Holy Spirit. I never got beyond the first question, which was, "Why did Jesus come?"

This may be a question easily answered, but the journey this question led me on became a wonderful adventure of discovering the intentionality of God and confirmed why I committed my life to Christ in the first place.

In Matthew chapter one, Joseph, Mary's betrothed, has a dream in which the Angel of the Lord comes to him and addresses his concern over Mary's pregnancy:

> *Joseph, son of David, do not be afraid to take to you Mary your wife, for that which is conceived in her is of the Holy Spirit. And she will bring forth a Son, and you shall call His name JESUS, for He will save His people from their sins* (Matthew 1:20-21).

Notice that the angel declares that Jesus "will save His people from their sins." Why was sin such an important issue that Jesus would leave eternity to confine Himself to time and space, put up with abuse from His own creation, and endure the Cross just to deal with it?

First of all, sin destroys life, both here and in eternity. Its very wage is death. Because He is love, God could not stand by and let sin destroy that which He created in His own image.

Second, God's intention from the beginning was fellowship with His creation, so He created a place where He could come and walk with the first couple in the cool of the evening. The saddest day in the history of man was the day that God entered the garden and saw that Adam and Eve were hiding from Him and He called out, "Adam, where are you?" Sin had brought a separation between man and God, and this was not acceptable to the Creator. Sin had to be dealt with so that man could fellowship with God.

Notice how Matthew interprets the event of Jesus' birth:

> *So all this was done that it might be fulfilled which was spoken by the Lord through the prophet, saying: "Behold, the virgin shall be with child, and bear a Son, and they shall call His name Immanuel," which is translated, "God with us"* (Matthew 1:22,23).

This prophecy of Isaiah places Jesus' coming in an experiential context. "God with us" does not refer to a message about God, but God in our midst, God to be known, God to be experienced.

I am thoroughly convinced that you cannot know God unless you experience Him. To experience means to "participate in personally." The word most often translated "to know" in Scripture is a Jewish idiom for sexual intercourse and refers to knowledge by experience. Jesus used this word when He made the statement, *"You shall know the truth, and the truth shall make you free*" (John 8:32). Many people intellectually know truth, but it is not liberating until they know that truth experientially.

A.W. Tozer, in the Preface of his book, *In Pursuit of God*, written in 1948, stated the following:

> Sound Bible exposition is an imperative must in the church of the Living God. Without it no church can be a New Testament church in any strict meaning of that term. But exposition may be carried on in such a way as to leave the hearers devoid of any true spiritual nourishment whatever. For it is not mere words that nourish the soul, but God Himself, and unless and until the hearers find God in personal experience they are not the better for having heard the truth. The Bible is not an end in itself, but a means to bring men to an intimate and satisfying knowledge of God, that they may enter into Him, that they may delight in His presence, may taste and know the inner sweetness of the very God Himself in the core and center of their hearts.[1]

As I mentioned earlier, Deborah was raised on the Monterey Bay in a quiet little fishing village by the name of Moss Landing. I first met her when I was nine years old and we grew up together in the same church. We were friends long before we became lovers.

On December 25, 1970, while traveling in my 1968 Mustang from Moss Landing to Santa Cruz, I nervously asked her to marry me, and she agreed. We were married nine months later on October 23, 1971. I have loved getting to know about Deborah. She has always been a bit of a mystery to me, and learning about the things she likes or dislikes, coming to understand her thinking and her emotions, and trying to see life through her eyes has been an amazing journey. As much as it has been an adventure getting to know these things about her, I didn't marry Deb for that primary purpose. I married her because she captivated my heart and I wanted to experience—to participate personally—life with her. To simply know about her was not an option.

Experiencing the manifest presence of God is as normal in the Kingdom of God as experiencing the presence of one's spouse. His presence is the essence of the Kingdom. Being possessed by His presence is our privilege as born-again people and is the absolute intention of God for us. He wants to be experienced, and He sealed this intention when He sent his Holy Spirit to be "God in us." If this were not so, He would have simply written a book and not bothered sending His Son or His Spirit.

We can study God, and gain a historical and intellectual knowledge of him. But we don't know Him until we personally experience Him.

We can study the Scripture, memorize it, and categorize it. We can even religiously run our life according to the principles of Scripture, but until we experience the living Word—Jesus, God with us—we have not discovered the true purpose of Scripture—to point us to a life experience with Christ.

Jesus made this plain to the Jews who loved to study the Scriptures when He stated:

You search the Scriptures, for in them you think you have eternal life; and these are they which testify of Me. But you are not willing to come to Me that you may have life (John 5:39,40).

All the wonderful expressions of the nature and character of God are only known through experience.

Take, for instance, God's love. We can study love, making ourselves aware of all the Greek words translated love—*phileo, eros*, even *agape*—but we can never know the love of God until He invades our hearts and we experience it.

The forgiveness of God is the same. It remains a concept until we participate in it. Without experiencing forgiveness, we stand on the outside looking in.

This is also true of the peace and goodness of God. His peace is only known when we enter His peace. Most people understand peace as the absence of conflict and battle. That's because they have not experienced it. When you have experienced the peace of God, you live in it irrespective of outward circumstances.

You can have an intellectual understanding that God is good—but until you identify that you have experienced a specific point of His goodness, you are left with theory and you will never fully trust your life to Him.

I have been accused, along with others at The Mission, of going after experience. It is with hand on heart that I declare to you in full confession that this is true. I am all about the manifest—felt, demonstrated, experienced—presence of God. It is true that I am out to experience everything about God that the Bible tells me I can—and it tells me that I can be filled with all the fullness of God and that I can know by experience the dimensions of His love, something that I can't know by intellectual pursuit. It tells me that I can expect to live in a dimension of life that is exceedingly abundant above all I can ask or think because that is the nature of the One who created me. It tells me that I can live supernaturally, demonstrating the Kingdom through signs, wonders, and miracles. Experiencing His presence is my inheritance, and I can settle for nothing inferior to this.

I didn't give my life to God because I was afraid of hell, or to get forgiveness for some gross sin. I was seven years old; what great sin could I have committed by that time in my life? I committed my life to God because I fell in love with Jesus Christ and was overwhelmed by the love of the Father. I could not resist the Holy Spirit-inspired internal yearning to know this One of such great love. The simple, yet profound answer to why Jesus came is so I can know Him.

As a community of people hungry for His presence, we at The Mission have decided that knowing about God without truly knowing Him and experiencing Him is meaningless. We cannot and will not settle for anything inferior to His manifest presence.

We have not come this far to stand at a distance while Jesus is saying "come." The objective of our warfare has not been for the destruction of the enemy but the embrace of the Father.

When my oldest granddaughter, Samantha, was about three years old, her mother brought her by our house to see her "Papa." Deborah was home, but I was at the church office. When Samantha stepped into the house, she stopped in the entrance, stood silent for a moment, and finally declared with both confidence and disappointment, "There's no Papa in this house." Samantha, a child with a very sensitive spirit, had measured the atmosphere and knew that I was not there. She then wanted to know where I was, for it was her Papa that she had come to see. A house without Papa was not the house she wanted to be in.

If there is no Papa in the church, no Papa in the vision, no Papa in the dream, no Papa in my destiny—then it's not a house I want to be in. It is a path I am not willing to follow.

As for me and my house, NIS finds its ultimate expression in the place of knowing Him, living in the rarified atmosphere of His presence.

Endnote

1. A.W. Tozer, *The Pursuit of God* (Harrisburg PA: Christian Publications Inc., 1948), p. 9.

About David Crone

David Crone
The Mission
6391 Leisure Town Road
Vacaville, California, 95687
Email: dcrone@tmvv.org
Website: Davecrone.com or Tmvv.org

In the right hands This Book will Change Lives!

Most of the people that need this message will not be looking for this book. To change their life you need to put a copy of this book in their hands.

> *But others (seeds) fell into good ground, and brought forth fruit, some a hundred-fold, some sixty-fold, some thirty-fold* (Matthew 13:3-8).

Our ministry is constantly seeking methods to find the good ground, the people that need this anointed message to change their life. Will you help us reach these people?

> *Remember this—a farmer who plants only a few seeds will get a small crop. But the one who plants generously will get a generous crop* (2 Corinthians 9:6).

EXTEND THIS MINISTRY BY SOWING
3-BOOKS, 5-BOOKS, 10-BOOKS, OR MORE TODAY,
AND BECOME A LIFE CHANGER!

Thank you,

Don Nori Sr., Publisher
Destiny Image
Since 1982